THE LI

THE LINK
The Extraordinary Gifts of a Teenage Psychic

MATTHEW MANNING

With a Preface by Peter Bander

COLIN SMYTHE
Gerrards Cross, Buckinghamshire

Copyright © 1973, 1987 by Colin Smythe Limited

First published in 1973 by Colin Smythe Limited, Gerrards Cross,
Buckinghamshire SL9 8XA
This edition first published in 1987
Reprinted in 1995

British Library Cataloguing in Publication Data
Manning, Matthew
    The link : the extraordinary gifts of
    a teenage psychic.
    1. Psychical research
    I. Title
    133.8'092'4   BF1028
    ISBN 0-86140-283-9

Produced in Great Britain
Printed and bound by The Guernsey Press Co. Ltd.,
Vale, Guernsey, C.I.

CONTENTS

ILLUSTRATIONS

PREFACE

Peter Bander

BY THE AGE of eighteen, when Matthew Manning wrote this book, he had experienced more psychic phenomena than most people hear about in a lifetime. Without apology for the skeptical approach I have maintained since I first met him, I consider his story to be more than just fascinating and totally absorbing; it is the record of a young man whom nature appears to have set aside from others.

Exactly what causes the many phenomena to manifest themselves in Matthew's presence is not certain. When I was writing the preface to the British edition of this book, various explanations abounded but none seemed even faintly conclusive. Sine publication of that edition, Matthew has submitted his unusual talents to serious and extensive scientific texts and experiments, the results of which shed some new light on his extraordinary gifts. In July 1974, a group of eminent scientists made some discoveries which not only appear to put Matthew's psychic abilities into perspective but also promise, after further evalution of the results, a revolution in psychical research and a hitherto undreamed-of explanation to many riddles and mysteries. In this new introduction, then, I have included as up-to-date an account as possible of the results of the latest experiments with Matthew.

When I was first approached by Matthew, there were those who sincerely believed that he should have gone instead to some esoteric sage who might have helped him to develop higher spiritual awareness and perhaps even trained him in the art of becoming a clairvoyant master. My own background—criminal psychology, theology, and pedagogics, a former senior lecturer at the Cambridge Institute of Education, and now a publisher was considered by some critics too materialistic and pragmatic for a young "sensitive", as they described him. Nevertheless, our partnership has, I believe, enriched both our lives and widened the horizon of our vision to a degree neither of us could have foreseen.

Matthew can be classed as an introvert. As a young child, his mother told me, he would absolutely refuse to talk to strangers. This was always attributed to extreme shyness. When he was scolded for misbehaviour, he would withdraw into a corner and remain there, sometimes, for hours, curled up in total isolation. He preferred his own company, and I have always found him reluctant to say more than appeared absolutely necessary. When asked to relate an incident, he will do so in such detail that one who does not know him personally may sometimes wonder whether he is telling a rehearsed story. He would make an excellent witness in court because he has a nearly perfect photographic memory and he is almost pedantic when relating an event or experience.

Matthew's own account of his family life, his schoolmates, his associates, and his actions and reactions during the turbulent years since the start of the psychic disturbances speaks for itself. Throughout my association with him, I have remained an outsider looking in. Naturally I formed my own opinions of Matthew, his parents, his teachers, and his schoolmates.

I do not envy Matthew his gifts and talents. As I have remarked, they have set him apart from his contemporaries. While others enjoyed friendship and shared the usual schoolboy excitements, Matthew was an object of curiosity, a stranger and often a person to be avoided because of his "strange powers". No doubt, distorted reports about what was happening at the school, rumours and fears of parents that their sons might catch whatever "affliction" Matthew had, contributed much to his predicament. Nonetheless, a small core of friends supported him throughout his school days. It is fair to say that he had only one intimate friend, whose understanding and deep affinity with Matthew have been a great help to him.

Matthew's strongest support and understanding came from his parents. They probably suffered more than Matthew realized at the time, yet their help was unstinting. In this age of egalitarianism, I would facetiously describe the circumstances of the Manning family as being slightly more equal than the average English family. The whole background is solid English middle class. For generations the Manning sons and daughters have received the best education. The Mannings own a very pleasant house, furnished in the finest English tradition. Matthew's father, Derek Manning, an architect of some standing and a collector of antique glass, emerges in Matthew's narrative as very much the *paterfamilias*, a no-nonsense man. Matthew's mother is a loving mother and friend to her three children.

It is against this family background that the chaos caused by the original poltergeist manifestations and later events must be seen; the Manning family is closely knit, and they naturally feared anything that could disturb the happiness and tranquillity of their homelife.

Apart from his parents, the two people most closely involved with

Matthew were his headmaster at Oakham school and the Matron of his school house. Both were, of course, *in loco parentis* while Matthew was resident at the school. The matron not only was sympathetic toward Matthew's gifts and delighted at the prospect of obtaining "first-hand evidence" for something she already believed in, but she had no doubt that Matthew was a natural medium and therefore a great comfort to her spiritual needs. Her role in the school and expecially her influence on the headmaster, who on two occasions wished Matthew to be withdrawn from the school because of the unbearable disturbances caused by poltergeistery and other phenomena, is not quite clear. But there can be little doubt that she used whatever influence she had to smooth Matthew's path. At the onset of the events related by Matthew, the headmaster began to receive second- and third-hand reports and complaints from the parents of many pupils and, no doubt, from members of his staff. One of Matthew's fellow pupils actually had to be withdrawn from the school because of the nervous strain caused by the nightly disturbances. Mr. J. D. Buchanan, the headmaster, gave the following statement to the press: "The things that happened when Matthew was at Oakham were simply mind-boggling. He must be the most unique boy I have met in twenty-eight years as a Master and Headmaster. Of course, I am a skeptic about psychic matters, but I know that something quite extraordinary was happening. I bent over backwards not to get involved, but I am sure there were paranormal powers at work to produce such mysterious happenings. I personally witnessed none of the happenings but plenty of people in his school house did. I had him under my personal care for about three years and I became very worried about all these happenings. There was never any explanation as to how all these disarrangements of dormitories etc. occurred. Knives, bricks, glass, pebbles and such like appeared without any clue as to their origin. And yet nothing ever appeared to be missing from other parts of the school. The boys who shared Matthew's dormitory and whose bunks moved about were absolutely adamant that it had happened; they were honest and nice boys and I know they did not tell lies. Yes, I decided to play the whole thing down as best I could, but something very odd was going on.

As to Matthew Manning himself, as a person he is a bit of a loner; he is rather lethargic, except at pottery at which he excelled. He was certainly not academically brilliant. His automatic paintings and drawings à la Dürer and other great Masters all seemed to sport their own identity and origin. Yet I know for a fact that Matthew really was not much good at drawing or painting. His art master was most impressed by the paintings purporting to be produced by the Great Masters."

My involvement with Matthew began a few months before he left the relatively sheltered environment of Oakham. I discussed with Mr. Derek Manning what possible future lay ahead for Matthew, and I suggested that it might not be a bad idea to give the young man a "rest from it all". Matthew agreed quite readily to get to work on an account of his last few years. I made it clear that I did not expect him to write the autobiography of an eighteen-year-old boy. Instead, I suggested that his narrative be restricted to the period from the onset of the psychic phenomena to the present. He was to come from Cambridge, where he lived, about once a fortnight to Gerrards Cross, where we would go through his manuscript chapter by chapter, and if necessary, line by line.

Of course, a multitude of questions arose in my own mind, and needless to say, many of my former academic colleagues asked me questions that I found very difficult to answer. I received a long letter from a respected friend, the doyen of parapsychological research in Britain, Dr. Robert Crookall, D.Sc., Ph.D., B.Sc., warning one of the terrible dangers of taking on a young man like Matthew Manning and allowing him to turn into a psychic freak; Dr. Crookall felt Matthew was far too young to be allowed to participate in experiments or pursue automatic writing and such matters.

My friends and colleagues were still asking whether Matthew was a *Wunderkind* or perhaps a special messenger from "the other side," and I was still trying to convince them that Matthew Manning was a normal, healthy, and intelligent young man who happened to possess some unusually strong paranormal gifts, when overnight something happened in Britain (and, we soon discovered, throughout the world) that caused us more trouble, inconvenience, and nuisance than had even the poltergeists. For some reason, television and the newspapers suddenly had one topic they flogged day after day, week after week: Mr. Uri Geller. No sooner had Mr. Geller appeared on television with his spoon- and key-bending performances than the questions we were asked changed: is Matthew Manning another Uri Geller?

As the weeks passed, the challenges forced upon Matthew, and to some degree on me, became even more demanding. In May 1974, I was contacted by an acquaintance who, I discovered later, is a high-ranking senior officer in the Special Branch (roughly analogous to the American FBI or CIA). He had seen photographs of Geller at Frankfurt Airport where Uri had purportedly caused a pair of Clejuso handcuffs to bend very slightly; as a matter of fact, opinion was divided whether or not they actually had bent. According to my acquaintance, this was prima facie evidence of fraud, because "these handcuffs are made of a special metal which does not bend". To prove his point, he

4

offered to have one pair delivered to my office the same afternoon.

I accepted, although in retrospect I think that was a mistake. The handcuffs were delivered at 3 P.M., and as Matthew happened to be in my office, he suggested that he put them on and I lock them. When nothing had happened by 4.30 P.M., I took them off Matthew, placed them in my briefcase, and took them home with me that evening. After dinner, Matthew came into my study and asked whether I could put the handcuffs around his wrists once again. "I have the feeling that something to going to happen," he said. While the handcuffs were tighly locked around his wrists, Matthew watched television. After an hour, my colleague Mr. Smythe, who, among others, was also present in the house, suggested taking the cuffs off Matthew because it was evident that the tight fit was causing him discomfort. The right cuff was released, but there was some difficulty with the left. Because Matthew assured us nothing had really happened (although he did feel very exhausted), we simply thought that the difficulty in releasing the cuff was due to our unfamiliarity with the key mechanism. We turned the key to the left cuff and nothing happened; we tried for about ten minutes, when I got impatient, blaming the manufacturers for inventing stupid devices that did not work properly. I then asked Matthew to come into a well-lighted room where I could see more clearly what I was doing. I noticed the bar that I had released fifteen minutes earlier from the right wrist had bent to about ten degrees. I tried to push the bar back into the lock but I could not manage even to press the bar back into the slot. I examined the handcuff on the left wrist. Inside the locking device, the notched bar had bent to what I estimated as some fifteen degrees.

I telephoned the gentleman and asked him to come to my house.

It would take too long to relate the happenings of the next two hours in detail; suffice it to say that after Matthew had been interrogated for about one hour, a way was found by which the circumference of the cuff was widened by about one and a half centimeters, without getting the locking bar out of position. The handcuffs were placed in a sealed envelope and taken personally by my acquaintance to the forensic laboratories of the Metropolitan Police, where they underwent the most stringent tests.

The report from the forensic laboratories was generously made known to me. We were given the X-ray photos of the metallurgical examinations. Making very technical references to the metal, its structure and molecular behaviour under stress, the report stated categorically that at no time had any physical force been brought to bear on these handcuffs. The only explanation that made any sense to the police forensic experts was that the handcuffs had been manufactured defective.

5

This event coincided with Matthew Manning's imminent departure for Toronto, Canada, where Dr. George Owen had convened a seminar that was to be attended by twenty-one leading scientists from the Western world. Dr. Owen, who had known Matthew since the first outbreak of the poltergeist phenomena in February 1967, had some time before left Cambridge University to be the director of the New Horizons Research Foundation in Toronto. He happily agreed to Dr. Owen's suggestion that Matthew should attend a special conference on psychokinesis in Toronto during the last two weeks of June and the first week of July 1974. In an agreement between Dr. Owen and myself it was specified that we would have full access to all research results and that a diary would be kept of all notable events during the experiments. Dr. Owen had agreed to send us a preliminary report and keep us generally informed by telephone from Toronto of any special happenings. Dr. Owen, must be given full credit for his imaginative and farsighted approach to the whole series of experiments that were carried out, and later published in a series of learned papers on Matthew Manning.

On October 8, 1974, I received the first official report from Toronto. Joel L. Whitton, M.D., research fellow, published a learned paper entitled *"Ramp Functions" in EEG Power Spectra During Actual and Attempted Paranormal Events*, and Dr. Owen published *A Preliminary Report on Matthew Manning's Physical Phenomena*. In the usual modest terminology of the great scientists, they state in a short preface: ". . . the result promises to lead to a new field of research whose interest may well extend beyond the merely parapsychology into more general realms of neurophysiological psychology. . . ."

Among the twenty-one giants of science who participated in the experiments with Matthew Manning was Professor Brian Josephson, F.R.S., Nobel prize recipient in physics (1973). Dr. Josephson has stated in an interview with the *Daily Mail* of London:

"We are on the verge of discoveries which may be extremely important for physics. We are dealing here with a new kind of energy. This force must be subject to laws. I believe ordinary methods of scientific investigation will tell us much about psychic phenomena. They are mysterious, but they are no more mysterious than a lot of things in physics already. In times past, "respectable" scientists would have nothing to do with psychical phenomena; many of them still won't. I think that the "respectable" scientists may find they have missed the boat!"

The *Daily Mail*'s literary editor followed Professor Josephson's remarks with the question:

To hear this from a professor of physics at Cambridge, speaking from that scientific holy of holies, the Cavendish Laboratory, makes psychic research seem a lot more impressive than it ever did before; and who could be more "respectable" than a professor of physics with a Nobel prize?

During the Toronto conference, a whole series of experiments was carried out with Matthew Manning. As the basis of my own narrative of events and discoveries, I use the diary the researchers kept at Toronto. Of necessity and for the purposes of this book, the facts and figures are simplified; I am also adding the theories, hypotheses, and even intelligent guesses that are in the diary. First the facts.

An initial series of eight experiements was carried out with Matthew Manning (followed by many other experiments involving different persons either alone or with Matthew present), during which Matthew was connected to an electroencephalograph and an electromyograph, and both devices were connected to a computer. After taking "normal" readings of Matthew's brain-wave pattern, both under relaxed conditions and while concentrating on some project, Matthew was instructed to "switch his power on". (I have questioned some of the scientists about using this peculiar phrase and was given to understand that Matthew had used the description of "switching power on" in conversation; the scientists simply adopted the phrase in order to discover what would happen if Matthew did switch his power on.) During the actual experiment, a key to a Canadian Dominion lock was placed into Matthew's hand, or alternately, he placed his hand above a key. The idea was to discover whether Matthew's brain wave would show any peculiar change during the operation.

As soon as Matthew complied with the instruction, the electroencephalograph registered an unexpected and quite unique reading. To all but one of the scientists present, the brain-wave pattern, registered each time for a period of twenty seconds, was entirely new. One of the medical professors present recalled having seen such a pattern once before in a patient to whom a severe overdose of a hallucinatory drug had been administered; the circumstances of that observation, however, had been such that no particular attention had been paid to its significance. I questioned not only the validity of the readings but also the description that had been given to this new brain wave: it was called a "ramp function". (Dr. Joel Whitton explained later that he had simply given a name to it so as to explain the situation to his fellow scientists. The actual EEG looks rather like a ramp, and "ramp function" was simply a pictorial description.)

During these experiments, the electromyograph showed no muscular activity whatsoever; one can therefore dispense with any further reference to this instrument. The readings from the computer, however, are interesting. According to the evaluation given in REM (rapid eye movement), Matthew had been in a fourth degree of deep sleep. It was quite obvious to the scientists present that Matthew had not been asleep—they could see he was wide awake. After twenty seconds, the ramp function stopped and the readings of Matthew's brain-wave pattern returned to normal. Some of the metal objects that had been placed under Matthew's hand had either bent or continued to bend afterward.

The second significant observation was made when the ramp function was traced back to the part of the brain from which it originated. We will have to await the written conclusions by some of the scientists who are most anxious that this discovery should be presented in an appropriate scientific evaluation. The only statement available is that the ramp function has been traced to a part of the human brain hitherto believed to be defunct and degenerated. The old "animal brain" of homo sapiens was one of the descriptions given, and "das Ur Gahirn" was another.

I think at this point it is appropriate to quote directly from Dr. Whitton's report.

The "ramp function" has not been reported previously; however, the large increase in theta energy and the usual decrease in beta energy which characterizes the ramp function compared to other states has been found by Motoyama (1965) to distinguish "paranormal" behaviour.

In test number 2 (MM2) there were two attempts at paranormal behaviour, i.e. MM attempted to bend two keys without using any obvious physical force. The second key did not bend and no ramp function was evidenced during the attempt with this key. A ramp function did appear, however, during the attempt with the first key during the first 10.24 seconds of the attempt. However, the first key did not bend until later in the experiment. It mysteriously bent while lying on a table in [an] adjoining room, but before the end of the experiment while MM was still "hooked up" to the EEG amplifier. MM claims this delayed effect occurs occasionally with metal objects he is "psychically" bending.

Summary

1. During the first 10 seconds of an attempt at paranormal behaviour by subjects with reportedly "psi" ability, the EEG power spectrum at the vertex demonstrates a form characterized as a ramp function.
2. The ramp is distinguished by a peak in the delta or low theta band, with most of the energy in the lower EEG frequencies with percentage theta twice that of beta.
3. Motoyama's (1965) finding of an increased theta energy in high scoring ESP subjects during paranormal behaviour is confirmed.
4. The ramp function does not appear to be related to the following

behaviours: resting eyes open, resting eyes closed, movements of muscles, talking, or intense concentration. The ramp function appears to be a unique physiological correlate of paranormal behaviour in the 3 psychics tested.

5. The ramp function was found in all three of the types of paranormal behaviour attempted: "psychokinesis," "projection," and "aura-viewing."

The discovery of the ramp function led immediately to a series of further experiments. Several persons reputed to be psychic were similarly tested. Following the tests, a number of theories and hypotheses were put forward by the scientists:

1. The origin of the ramp function (and therefore the source of psychic energy) in Matthew was found to be in the oldest part of the human brain; Dr. Whitton therefore suggests that psychic ability of energy is not a "random gift" or a "space-age ability", but an innate function and ability in homo sapiens that probably goes back to the earliest history of man; it may be a function that became lost or defunct in most people many thousands of years ago.

2. The psychic energy level recorded in Matthew was exceptionally high—in fact, unique. Two questions must be asked: why is Matthew's energy level so much higher than that of other known psychics? And, is there a common factor among psychics that accounts for the functioning of this "old and defunct" part of the brain? (Preliminary evaluations of questionnaires may point to a solution, but it would be premature to place too much reliance on the results obtained so far. I shall, however, comment on his problem below.)

3. A nonpsychic can be given psychic powers and ability through biofeedback. It should therefore be possible to utilize the brain waves from Matthew, which have been stored in the computer memory bank, and transfer them at a later time to a nonpsychic. (Such experiments will surely be performed by some scientists in the future.)

4. The ramp function produced by Matthew during the experiments is totally different from readings obtained during "moments of concentration", for example. It can therefore be surmised that psychic ability, although innate, is *not* a higher or different degree of concentration but it suggests an unknown outside or inside force which creates it.

Of course, the startling findings in Toronto lend themselves to speculation; there is no end to the suggestions and theories they gave rise to. One of them may be correct. The one theory put foward by Dr. Noel Whitton (purely as a working hypothesis) is the result of an investigation carried out on a very small scale. A number of known psychics had been asked by Dr. Whitton to fill in a questionnaire.

Their answers to questions about personal experiences during early childhood showed several of the psychics had one experience in common. The answer Matthew supplied is most fascinating. The common experience of the psychics was simply that they all had suffered a severe electric shock before the age of ten. Matthew did not recall any such accident; it was only when we talked about this with Matthew's parents that we learned Matthew's mother had suffered such a severe electric shock three weeks before Matthew was born that she feared she might lose Matthew.

Among the other experiments carried out on Matthew in Toronto were those by Dr. Douglas Dean with Kirlian photography. According to Dr. Dean, "The apparatus consists of a Testa coil generator or electronic leak tester which gives about 25,000 volts a.c. at about 100,000 to 1,000,000 frequency in cycles per second with about 50 pulses per second."

"The results I have obtained with Matthew Manning are absolutely unique," Dr. Dean stated afterwards. "I have never seen anything like this before."

There has been a sequel to these experiments. Following the enthusiastic statements by Dr. Dean, I was approached by a group of electronics experts from the Netherlands and Germany. Aura Electronics of Holland recently developed a most advanced Kirlian apparatus generating 35,000 volts and allowing photographs of considerably larger areas to be taken. We arranged a short session for September 4, 1974, and Matthew Manning was asked once again to "switch his power on". Having made it quite clear to me that "this kind of result could never be reproduced on our machines because they are far superior to anything available in the world", the three electronics experts left England in considerable distress: two of their Kirlian machines had broken down when they had invited Matthew "to put all the energy he had into the machine".

Mr. M. H. J. Th. van der Veer, head of the research group, issued the following statement afterwards:

"After experiments with over one thousand subjects, we are completely baffled by the results. Not only are the Kirlian photographs we took totally different from anything we have ever seen, but this young man appears to possess the ability of generating his own energy which just cancels out the 35,000 volts of the machine. In fact, I am not quite sure about what really happened; at one moment, he seemed to absorb the total energy from the machine, and at the next, he forced such an energy back into the machine that the machines just "gave up their ghost". If we had not seen this with our own eyes, we would not have believed this possible. I can state categorically that in order to do what Matthew did by simply placing his hand on the Kirlian machine, one would need highly sophisticated electronic equipment."

Finally, I ought to mention one of the experiments which, for reasons of scientific accuracy, must be described as inconclusive. Dr. Brian Josephson carried out an experiment with a compass in which Matthew placed his hand above the compass and the needle spun violently. When Matthew "switched off" his energy, the needle, instead of swingin slowly back and forth until it came to rest, suddenly stopped dead. Since Professor Josephson thought the humidity in the room may have had an effect on the needle's behaviour, he preferred to label the results "inconclusive". During subsequent experiments at the Cavendish Laboratory in Cambridge, however, the same effect on the needle was observed. At the same time it was discovered that Matthew's energy affected the magnetic field of the compass. Instruments designed to measure changes in magnetic fields were situated several yards away from the compass, and as Matthew switched his power on above the needle, the instruments registered a change. When Matthew walked over to the instruments, they again immediately registered a change in magnetic field around the compass, but the needle of the compass remained stationary. Professor Josephson could find no rational explanation for the behaviour of the compass needle and the instruments; unless he can prove that Matthew Manning either influenced the compass needle or the instruments, and until the nature of Matthew's energy output can be defined scientifically, as a physicist he feels compelled to label such results "inconclusive".

Seen in the light of the Toronto results, Matthew Manning's book takes on a new and unexpected significance. Matthew's gifts are still mysterious and fascinating, but the "spook" has gone out of them. While Matthew and his extraordinary abilities will probably occupy scientific research for some years to come, let us in the meantime also realize that Matthew's contribution, especially in Toronto, may put a firm and final end to the rampant fantasies about psychic gifts.

Today we can say that to be psychic simply means to be able to utilize a faculty that is latent in each of us.

Toronto has not supplied an answer or solution to the most important question: does Matthew, when he "switches his power on", communicate with anybody? All the apperances indicate that he does. I, for one, would like to know why Picasso, Dürer, Bertrand Russell, and hundreds of men and women known to be dead, would want to communicate through an eighteen-year-old schoolboy.

This is a most unsatisfactory end to the introduction; I would have preferred to present an open-and-shut case. I only hope that the knowledge gained through the Toronto experiments and all desires to learn more will not be dispersed to play havoc among mankind. On the

11

contrary, I share Matthew's wish that whatever we learn in the next few years will benefit man and help toward a better world—here and hereafter.

P.B.

Gerrards Cross
Buckinghamshire, England
October 1974

INTRODUCTION

SHORTLY AFTER the war I read Harry Price's book *Poltergeist over England*. I was already acquainted with *An Adventure* by the Misses Moberly and Jourdain and these two volumes were the basis of any imperfect understanding of the supernature I possessed. At that time I could not forsee that a generation later I should be introducing an account of experiences far stranger, more persistent and diverse than any which Harry Price was able to recount. The narrative which follows has an added immediacy because the victim (and I believe any poltergeist-child *is* an unwitting victim) is in this case my son. I am grateful for the information I obtained and remembered from Price's book: without it the phenomenon which began to uncoil might have remained unrecognized far longer, and the anxiety which it provoked have been more serious for my family.

The household in which the events originally took place in 1966 had one characteristic common to most poltergeist cases: children. Andrew was six, Rosalind aged eight and the eldest (the author) just eleven. None of them could comprehend the nature of the situation and this factor undoubtedly increased their apprehension. As the events persisted I became aware of certain characteristics which the force revealed. This poltergeist was a silent operator and not to be caught red-handed. It was teasingly just that much faster and far-seeing than humans, and the realisation of this increased the sense of frustration and helplessness.

In retrospect the arrival of Dr. George Owen was coincidental, but his range of experience of the subject was unrivalled and he provided the psychological assurance which my family needed at that time. We were especially comforted by his confidence that the phenomenon was transitory, was expendable, would go away. In this he was correct. When the activities resumed five years later everyone was more experienced, desiring only to live undisturbed and in peace, but this wish was to be tempestuously upset.

The forces displayed during the second outbreak were considerably more intense, mischievous and daring. I believe they deserved far more serious and scientific an examination than, in fact they received and I am convinced there were clues undetected which, if they had been followed, may well have advanced one's understanding of the dynamics and motives of poltergeist energy.

The reader of *The Link* will at some point have to evaluate the evidence and decide upon its veracity and probability. I know the author has no intent to convince the incredulous nor wish to deceive the sympathetic. It is a *description* by a young man who has been at the centre of experiences so exceptional that they could not be allowed to remain unrecorded.

My personal attitude throughout, I trust, was to be open-minded, which is all a layman can be. There was no other choice than to respond to events as they occurred, but inevitably I developed a heightened awareness of the situation. I became more observant and testing and looked always for the *sensible* explanation of events. Later I realized that if I was to assess the probability of the evidence my choice was unequivocal: either I rejected *in toto* the paranormal explanation of events or I accepted them. (Even to dismiss 98% as exuberant pranks would leave a crucial 2% unexplained to challenge my judgment.) The first option became increasingly untenable and less rational than acceptance of the alternative.

It is a reflection of the responsibility with which people today treat psychic phenomena to record the unexpected degree of social acceptance by people who were acquainted with our situation. An overwhelming, and unexpected, majority accepted (I believe sincerely) our accounts of poltergeist activity, dematerializations and spirit activity to which we had been subjected. Matthew himself quickly appreciated his responsibility to his family, his school, and to those motivated by desire to understand, and to scientific enquiry. Few of us perhaps realized the unique burden that he has carried. I am proud to record the sense of dignity with which he has faced his destiny and earnestly trust that he will possess the fortitude to continue.

I hope the reader will find material of interest in *Open To Suggestion* and appreciate the youthful extent of the author's literary experience. If this Introduction stimulates enquiry then it is no secret that this narrative is itself an introduction to a far larger story.

Derek G. Manning
October, 1975

14

CHAPTER I

I HAD always looked forward to going back to school after my holidays. It was not that I was unhappy, but I very much enjoyed the company of my school friends, not knowing many people at home.

My Easter holidays were over and on Sunday I was getting ready for my journey back to school; my father was going to accompany me because he had requested an interview with my Headmaster. The thought of what might result from this interview worried me very much, but then my father had been a very worried man for some time and my family had reached a breaking point. For the last four weeks we all had been subjected to the most disturbing and sometimes frightening happenings in the house. Just to describe them as psychic phenomena does not capture the dismay my parents, my younger brother and sister had lived through. There is no doubt that I was at the very root of all that had happened.

In view of these extraordinary phenomena, my father thought it only fair to inform the Headmaster that in his own opinion—and he was proven right—there was a possibility that such phenomena might occur after I had returned to school. Judging by the disturbances happening to those who were closest to me, he assumed that if similar occurrences should take place at my school, the disturbances might have far more devastating effects than they had in my home.

On Sunday night my father and I left Cambridge by car for my school. I do not know whether I felt sorry for myself or for my father, and we had not even left the outskirts of Cambridge when we talked about some of the things that had happened, trying to make sense of them and somehow finding an explanation which might satisfy the Headmaster, and prepare me for this ordeal which my father anticipated and I feared.

It had all started on the morning of 18th February, 1967, early on a grey Saturday morning, when my family witnessed for the first time phenomena that began suddenly for no apparent reason, and appeared to cease just as suddenly at Easter that year.

We were occupying at that time a recently-built detached house, and had lived there for seven years. Being a reasonably modern house it had an open style, and contained several ground to ceiling windows.

Our house ran to a predictable and orderly routine; but suddenly this was no longer the case. Over-night the pattern of living was disrupted.

My father used to begin his day by opening up the grate of the all-night burning fire at 7 a.m., to add fuel to it. Afterwards he would go back upstairs to the bathroom and come down to the living room at about 7.25 a.m.

He did so on 18th February, a Saturday. Lying on its side, on the floor, he discovered a silver tankard that was usually kept on a wooden shelf $4\frac{1}{2}$ feet from the floor. He was surprised to find that it was not damaged, even though directly beneath the shelf was a cupboard; the tankard would have had to have hit this if it had fallen of its own accord.

My younger brother and sister and myself were all questioned about this at breakfast. No one accepted responsibility for the tankard and all denied any knowledge of it.

Naturally enough we immediately thought that we had been burgled during the night. This idea was soon dispelled when we found that no other objects were missing. It would not have been easy for a burglar to have broken in at night, anyway, without the risk of waking someone. The event was forgotten.

On the following Wednesday morning, my father found the tankard again lying on its side on the floor, under identical circumstances. Once again each member of the family pleaded innocence; jokingly we all accused one another, although we knew that my father was always the first to come downstairs and enter the room; in fact he woke up the rest of us each day.

We were by now a little curious and puzzled as to the cause of the tankard's apparently inexplicable movement. There was no reason for it: the shelf was of well seasoned, planed and polished wood, and was perfectly horizontal. We kept no pets that could have displaced it, and the shelf was not sited near any fireplace or flue.

The tankard was surrounded that night by a ring of sprinkled talc, placed there, unknown to myself or my brother and sister, by my parents. If the tankard subsequently slid horizontally towards the edge of the shelf and the floor, the powder would provide evidence of this by being disturbed.

The powder ring was still intact when the tankard was found on the floor the next morning. It must, therefore, have risen vertically and then horizontally to achieve such a position without disturbing the powder. Furthermore, this piece of amateur detective work seemed to have encouraged the person who moved the tankard.

My mother, glancing at the table, laid the night before for breakfast, noticed a large flower-filled vase had been placed on the mat where we normally put the teapot. The vase had been moved from the opposite end of the room, some twenty feet, without spilling any of the water. I then found an old pottery dog conspicuously repositioned above the fireplace, having moved five feet from its position on a nearby shelf.

It was now that for the first time we suspected that some freakish happenings were taking place; our feelings were mixed. We did not know whether to laugh or cry. We had no idea what might happen next, or what counter-action we could take, as it was totally outside our field of experience. Obviously none of us had ever encountered such happenings before, and although it was amusing in its impishness, it frightened us because we were not acquainted with it, and were unaware of its limits and purpose. We could not understand why this should suddenly happen; there seemed no discernible cause.

Feeling that some form of counter-action was necessary, my father's next problem was finding out what could be done and who might be able to help us. He tried the doctor and the police. It was the latter, who although very sympathetic but unable to offer an assistance, advised him to approach the Cambridge Psychical Research Society.

Following their advice, he got in touch with its Secretary, Dr. George Owen, who was an expert on poltergeist phenomena. He was at this time a Fellow of Trinity College, Cambridge, lecturing in Genetics.

Dr. Owen informed us that such outbreaks were often associated with the presence of children, that their duration was generally two to eight weeks, and that once they ceased, would not recur. He was unable to suggest any preventive measures, but assured us that the scientific interest outweighed the inconveniences these events occasioned.

As Dr. Owen could offer no "cure" for the phenomena, my father wrote to another university expert, at a provincial university, describing briefly the events, and concluding, "that this activity is apparently increasing".

"We have three children," my father wrote, "Matthew aged eleven years six months, Rosalind, eight years seven months, and Andrew, seven years old, and although they may be indirectly responsible for these occurrences, I am reasonably certain that the physical movement of these articles is not their work.

"I am an interested student of antiques and our room accommodates a number of my acquisitions, most of which could be broken by dropping. It is therefore particularly gratifying to observe that in the main fragile objects are undisturbed! A basket containing ornamented gourds which has twice been moved weighs two and three-quarter pounds.

"The general effect of these movements suggests a sense of impish mischief allied with a careful sense of order, and so far my family are outwardly taking the matter fairly light-heartedly. It is possible, however, that the results are perhaps psychologically more disturbing, and for this reason I should be relieved to see these episodes concluded." The letter was never answered.

With similar happenings continuing and increasing in intensity, the phenomena appeared to get more powerful. They became a daily routine and always took place between 7.00 a.m. and 7.30 a.m.; this period covered half an hour when the family was in a semi-conscious state, just awaking.

From the top of the stairs it was possible to hear knocks and other sounds as the upheavals increased, but we did not witness any of these objects in flight. Invariably the objects which were moved were light-weight ornaments, chairs, cutlery, ashtrays, baskets, plates, a small coffee table and a score of other articles, but none was ever broken or spilled. The tankard was regularly moved; we wondered if it was perhaps some form of defiant protest against my father, since it was his tankard, and he alone drank from it. Also a vase of flowers would frequently be brought and placed on the breakfast table, in front of where my mother sat.

On one occasion my father entered the living room early, before any disturbances had taken place, and put in the room a transistor radio playing music. This appeared to have a deterrent effect, as the phenomenon was not as strong as had been previously experienced.

As the physical manifestations increased, the house began to produce erratic and unsuspected taps and creaks. The noises would vary from a dull knocking to a sound like a small stone being thrown at the window, and they continued throughout the day and night in all parts of the house.

On several occasions at night all the doors and openings into the living room were sealed by cotton threads which would be snapped if anyone entered the room; and the staircase was similarly booby trapped. It appeared that nothing could be attributed to human mischief as the threads remained intact but the room was again disturbed.

Dr. Owen and my father watched the room from the outside on

(*Above*) Derek Manning, Matthew's father, discovered the first object which was moved, a Georgian silver tankard.

(*Left*) Matthew shortly after the first outbreak of poltergeist activity on 18 February, 1967;

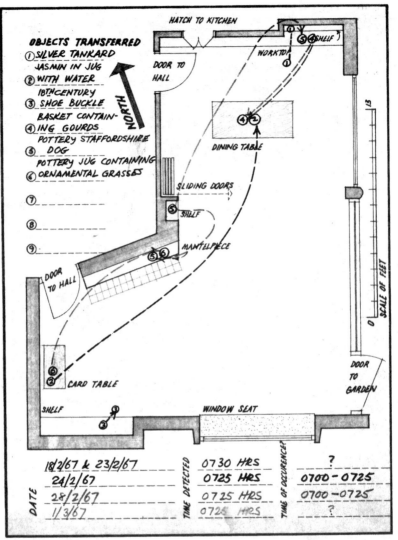

The sudden and completely unexpected poltergeist occurrences were not immediately recognised as such. Only after Mr. Manning had taken every precaution to make it impossible for anybody to get near the objects which were mysteriously moved about the rooms between 7 and 7.30 in the mornings, did he suspect that the cause of the disturbances was of paranormal origin. The police were unable to give any advice or assistance and suggested that Mr. Manning get in touch with the Cambridge Society for Psychical Research. Dr. George Owen, a lecturer in genetics at Trinity College and secretary of the C.S.P.R., investigated the poltergeist outbreak.

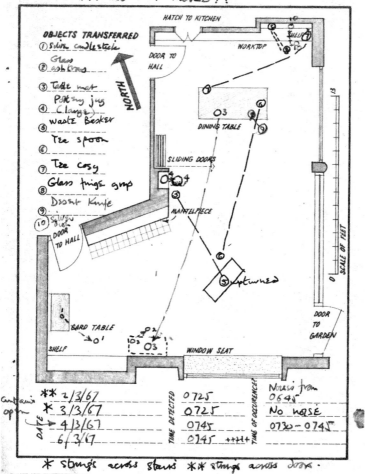

Mr. Manning, an architect with a Regional Hospital Board, assisted Dr. Owen in preparing Movement Charts on which all moving objects were recorded. It soon became clear that the objects would only move when nobody was in the room. When Dr. Owen arrived unannounced at the Manning house in Shelford, Cambridge, he took up an observation point outside at 6.15 in the morning from which he could see clearly into the sitting room. When nothing had happened by 7.15, he walked quickly to the door and discovered that several objects had been moved in the 30 seconds it had taken him to enter the room which had been securely closed with a series of cotton threads fastened across the doorway. These would have to be broken or cut to gain entry.

21

Dr. George Owen: *"My opinion is that the happenings are genuine, and not caused by trickery, that the house was not haunted, and that the events were P.K. (psycho-kinesis) caused by a member of the household. Matthew was the most likely one on the grounds of age, although there was no other factor to indicate that especially."*

After further extensive examinations Dr. Owen came to the conclusion that "the force, whatever it may be, resides principally in Matthew."

more than one occasion, and they found that during these times no phenomena could be witnessed. As soon as they relinquished their positions however, the objects would begin to move as if they were aware only to well of when they were being watched.

In order to really double-check to the best of his ability that these movements were not spurious, Dr. Owen arrived one morning without warning, to watch the room by himself. He even took the trouble of leaving his car some distance away and walking the last part so that he could take up position unseen at about 6.30 a.m. While he watched no object was seen to move, and neither did anyone enter the room. As soon as he ceased watching, to come round to the front door, the small objects again began to move.

On March 6th at George Owen's suggestion, my brother, my sister and myself were all sent to stay in different friends' houses for a week. Although my parents had no difficulty in finding friends to have Rosalind and Andrew to stay, they had great difficulty in finding anyone who was willing to have me under their roof. Even by this stage it appeared that I was being regarded as the person around which this force centred, principally because of my age, although I was not made aware of this fact.

However, during that time we spent away from home, no movement took place around my parents or myself, or my brother and sister, but the noises were still audible to my parents at home during all hours of the day. This experiment did appear to prove that the force resided in one of us three children.

As if to make up for lost time, when we returned we were greeted on the first morning by a fresh outbreak executed with renewed vigour. On 13th March nine objects moved between 7.00 a.m. and 7.30 a.m., and although that may not have been an extraordinarily large number, the objects increased in size, so that an upholstered chair moved about six feet, a dining chair was upturned, a candlestick was placed in the middle of a vase of flowers,, and other small objects moved.

A peak in the physical manifestations was reached on the following morning, when eleven objects were moved during fifteen minutes. From that day on there appeared to be a waning of the movements; small objects moved shorter distances. We had been witness to this poltergeist for nearly three months, and although we had not noted other characteristics occasionally found in similar cases, such as fire-raising and smell-producing, the other hallmarks of a poltergeist were unmistakable. Dr. Owen had warned my father about these possibilities.

The last event that occurred was of particular interest, and it was unlike anything else we had previously experienced. Seated on a settee, my sister had been drawing, with her work on her knees; she had made a mistake, and wanting to correct it, she looked for her rubber, which she had used earlier, but now seemed lost. She sat alone in the living room, as I entered it. I stopped dead in my tracks as I saw rising behind her a rubber, ascending slowly from behind the settee on which she sat. At the same moment as I saw it, she too caught sight of it. It rose about five feet from the floor, hung in the air, and slowly floated down to land beside her. Although it was her lost rubber, we were terrified for the first time and rushed from the house.

One event that assured us that the force resided not in our house but in a member of the family took place in another house, some twenty miles away. On arriving at my grand-parents' home one Sunday, my mother placed her coat upstairs, laid flat on a bed. When we came to leave and my mother went to fetch her coat, she found it arranged on the floor at the side of the bed, in the same manner as it had been left on the bed. Although my grand-parents would not hear of our explanation, we realised that it was probably one of those poltergeist manifestations.

In many ways the most interesting aspect of the phenomenon was a "pinging" sound that we often heard; it seemed to rebound off windows or radiators, and occasionally glass or china; although it sounded like tiny beads striking these objects, the sound was similar to that made by a bat. It occurred to us that the poltergeist was perhaps employing a technique comparable to that of a bat, in negotiating articles through the air and round corners; was it possible that on much the same principle as a bat uses an echo-sounding device to avoid obstacles, the poltergeist was using similar methods?

I had in my bedroom the skull of a monk, which I had removed from the subsiding cliff that had once supported a medieval monastery. Thinking that this was a cause of this episode, the skull was duly buried (under the nearest tree), but it made no difference to the intensity of the happenings.

Another interesting occurrence befell my father on more than one occasion. Being asleep at night, he would be awakened suddenly for no apparent reason. He was not in a drowsy state, but perfectly alert and aware of everything going on around him. He had the feeling that a cat was moving on top of his bedclothes, up and down his legs, trying to find a comfortable position in which to settle down. After it had apparently done so, he would feel a weight on his feet, although there was no cat. Having experienced this on more occasions

24

than he cared for, he obtained some sleeping pills from the doctor, and he no longer woke up during the night.

The reaction of the family was initially one of fright, but gradually we began to joke about it, and we could see an amusing side to it all, which I think was of great help to us all. People are always frightened of happenings they cannot understand, and this was our situation. On the other hand, people who cannot comprehend something will often reject it. But what was there to reject in our case? Such undeniable evidence of moving objects could not be rejected and dismissed as if they had been imagined. We tried to understand it but, I admit, we were not very successful. We felt isolated because we knew no one else who had any similar experience and who might have been able to help us. We were seized with a sense of always having to look over our shoulders to see if we were going to get hit, although this never happened. My mother was reluctant to stay in the house on her own at this time, and would wander aimlessly around the nearest town.

Soon after the last event with the rubber, we left for an Easter holiday, which happened to serve as a very useful break, as it took our minds off the subject. On our return three weeks later all was quiet again, as it had been before 18th February.

The following extract is taken from a letter subsequently written by Dr. Owen:

". . . thank you for your careful description of the events surrounding Matthew. In the haunting . . . at your previous home . . . my opinion was that the happenings were genuine, and not caused by trickery, that the house was not haunted, and that the events were P.K. (psycho-kinesis) caused by a member of the household. It was not possible at that time to ascertain which member of the family was the source of the force. Matthew was the most likely on the grounds of age, although there was no other factor to indicate this especially. His obvious intelligence, pleasant nature, and underlying seriousness were, of course, quite typical of other poltergeist people, but these characteristics were shared by the rest of your family. At one time I wondered if Mrs. Manning was the unconscious involuntary source of the force, as occasionally it is manifested by older persons, but this was only because she was the one who seemed outwardly to be the most tense. However, in these things it is obviously hard to separate cause and effect.

"I think you can assume that the present occurrences are not due to your house being "haunted" at all. The force, whatever it may be, resides principally in Matthew."

I might say here that Dr. Owen is a well qualified and experienced researcher with a strict scientific approach to parapsychology. He won, in 1963, The Treatise Award of the Parapsychology Foundation, and the following year was awarded the Duke University prize for distinguished work in parapsychology. His scientific papers have also been published in such learned and prestigious journals as "Proceedings of the Royal Society". In 1970 he accepted an invitation to become the Director of The New Horizons Research Foundation, in Toronto.

At the time the poltergeist phenomena was occurring I was due to sit the Common Entrance Examination which would determine which school I was to go to after I had left preparatory school, and I was very tense. I believe that this may have been a contributory factor to the outbreak of the phenomenon in the first place, and that because of the tension I felt, I was generating "energy" which was helping to cause the poltergeist activity.

After the examination I left my preparatory school in 1968 and in September I entered a large public school. In the autumn of 1968 we also moved and bought an old house some eight miles away from our previous home. The reason for the move had nothing to do with the poltergeist and it was not because we thought our house was haunted. I settled into the new school and the family into a new house. The events that had made such havoc of our lives disappeared into the past and were soon forgotten.

It is common for schoolboys to have "crazes" on something, usually for a short period of time, and this is all everybody talks about while it is fashion. One such "craze" that swept my classmates in my house at school, late in 1969, was holding seances, which in retrospect I think was a stupid thing to have engaged in.

We adopted several methods of communication with varying degrees of success. This also depended a great deal on who was taking part in the seance, and I remember that a number of my friends cheated. Even so, some results are worth mentioning. We tried these seances with different combinations of operators and some of the best results seemed to be achieved when I was one of the team. Although the messages we received were largely garbled and made little sense to any of us, my presence was usually a guarantee for something "coming through" without cheating.

One of the most striking happenings took place when three of us tried to contact the grandfather of one of the boys, who although present, was not actually taking part in the seance. He wanted us to find out from his grandfather where he died. This boy knew the place but we did not. The name spelt out was RAVENSGLASS, which was the correct answer. This could of course be explained by telepathy.

Other results were perhaps not quite so impressive and were largely of the type: "James warns you not to do this. You are putting your lives at risk." We also received our fair share of messages purporting to be from Marie Antoinette and Winston Churchill! When the "other side" was asked why better results were achieved when I was involved in the experiment the reply spelt out was FREDERICK WHITE, which was the name of my grandfather who had died some eleven years previously.

However, this "craze" for seances changed after most people had become too frightened to continue.

For nearly a year after this nothing unusual occurred and 1970 was a quiet year. At that time I took two English "O" levels. The remainder of my "O" levels were due to be taken during the summer of 1971, so that by the end of 1970 I had six "O" levels left to be taken.

The spring and summer terms in 1970 passed without disturbance and the poltergeist of three years ago was forgotten. After all, Dr. Owen had told us on more than one occasion that poltergeists never returned.

Early in July 1970 the school closed for the summer holidays and I returned home.

On July 17th, a few days into the summer holidays, my parents bought an antique wardrobe for my bedroom, which was on the ground floor. It was a very heavy large oak wardrobe, and because of its size it had at one time been cut in half down the middle to make it possible to move it. As soon as it was placed in my room I got an odd feeling from it; I liked it and at the same time I felt there was something very wrong with it, probably because it had been cut through the middle. However, I hung up my clothes, and closed the doors. There were two doors which made up its front, and one of these doors had bolts to secure it at the top and bottom; the other door had a key-operated lock which closed the cupboard firmly. I shut and locked it and left the room.

Returning to the room some minutes later to fetch something, I found both doors hanging open; I bolted and locked them again. I could not immediately see any reason for the doors opening on their own, as both halves of the cupboard were screwed firmly together. I again left the room, with the wardrobe doors firmly locked.

Half an hour later, when I returned, both doors were again wide open. I accounted for it by the two halves not fitting together properly, and again locked the doors with the two bolts and the key.

After closing the doors and checking that I could not open them when they were locked, I put the key in my pocket so that nobody else could open them either. This procedure did not prevent the doors from opening, after I continued to lock them, but they would only open if I was not watching them. I told my parents of the trouble I was having in keeping the doors closed, and I was met with a negative, uninterested response, and did not therefore say more about it.

This trouble continued for several weeks until I returned to school in September. While I was at school nothing odd occurred and I had soon forgotten the cupboard. Although I was suspicious of the cause of the opening of the doors, I did not think that it was another poltergeist.

I returned home for a weekend about four weeks later and when I first entered my room the cupboard doors were closed. Having left the room, I returned later to find both doors open. I shut them and sat down with my back to the cupboard, listening to a record. After about fifteen minutes a boot hit the window, about ten feet in front of me, and I found both cupboard doors wide open; the boot had come from the cupboard. I said nothing to anybody about this and the rest of the weekend passed without further disturbance.

Four weeks later I returned home for a week's half-term break. The wardrobe doors were still up to their usual tricks, and other small objects started to move about the room as well. I still did not say anything to my parents, having met with a stony response to my telling them about the wardrobe some time ago. Cushions began to take on a life of their own, moving from one side of the room to the other.

When I returned to school I told one or two of my friends about the happenings, and decided that next time I came home I would take a camera and a tape recorder. The phenomenon was still being limited to the house and nothing happened at school.

I brought home a Polaroid camera and a battery-operated tape recorder when I returned three weeks later, so that I could record on film and perhaps on tape some of the phenomena that seemed to take place in my bedroom.

I was not disappointed and quite soon after arranging my camera and tape recorder, the cupboard doors opened and a boot "hurled" itself towards the window. I followed the path of the boot with my camera for as long as possible, trying to get a good picture, and just

In November 1968 the Manning family moved to Linton near Cambridge. Queen's House became the centre of further outbreaks of poltergeist phenomena when they started again in 1971.

(Left) Front of Queen's House; Matthew standing outside the bedroom where over five-hundred "spirit graffiti" appeared on the walls.

(Below) Built in 1731, there are several features to the building which made the government issue a preservation order for Queen's House. The white buildings towards the back were built in 1600 or earlier.

29

In *August* 1971 *apports began to appear on the landings and staircases. Among these objects was a loaf of bread, the age of which was guessed to be about seventy years; an old bee's wax candle; fossils, a string of beads and objects which did not belong in the house. Every member of the Manning household found, at one time or other, strange objects. They always materialised when nobody was in the vicinity of the staircase or landing. Apports also appeared at Matthew's school; this phenomenon has never ceased.*

Mrs. Manning has, on occasions, been subjected to severe poltergeist disturbances. At one time Dr. Owen wondered if Mrs. Manning was the unconscious involuntary source of the force, but this was only because she was the one who seemed outwardly the most tense.

(Below) During a severe "attack" the dining and sitting rooms were put in total disarray many times during one morning.

Rosalind, Matthew's sister, was eight years old when the first outbreak of poltergeist phenomena occurred, and eleven at the time of the second series of manifestations, in 1971. Although frightened and unwilling to be in the house by herself, she, like the other members of the family, got used to living in rooms from which objects disappeared. A table in her room disappeared and was found two floors down in the cellar with all objects on it still in position.

The walls in Queen's House attracted a special kind of attention. Apart from the graffiti in the bedroom, large signatures, short incoherent sentences and drawings appeared everywhere. Even the high ceilings were not safe from pencil drawings and scribbles. Often the writing is upside down. In the beginning, large childish scribbles, approximately six inches in diameter, appeared everywhere.

(Left) The first marks were detected next to the barometer in the dining room.

managed to photograph it as it dropped towards the floor; I failed to get the whole boot into the picture because of the speed at which it was falling. Even though the tape recorder picked up very few sounds, I succeeded in photographing a book as it flew across the room.

Three weeks later the end of term arrived and I came home for four weeks Christmas holiday. The movements started in my bedroom almost as soon as I got home, but it seemed that nothing was happening anywhere outside it. This began to get irritating, because I was the only person being subjected to these happenings and nobody else was interested or believed me. The phenomenon did at least limit itself to small objects like cushions or coat-hangers, and I therefore persuaded myself that there might be a natural explanation for these small movements. This gave me some sort of comfort. Disturbances would occur at intervals throughout the day when I was in the room on my own.

Early on Christmas morning I was awoken by an unusual noise from behind the panelling on the other side of the room. It sounded to me like a cat scratching the panelling from the inside. This continued for some minutes and then faded away, to be followed by a noise from just outside the window which sounded like someone walking backwards and forwards on gravel. This stopped, and when I looked out of the window, I saw that the snow on the ground showed no footprints; in fact there was no gravel there either which I thought strange. By the time I was back in bed again the scratching was coming from behind the panelling again.

While it was still audible I fetched my mother downstairs, so that she too could hear the sound. As if to deliberately defy me, the room was quiet when we got downstairs and my mother refused to believe that any such noises had occurred. Having again met with such a response, I decided not to mention the subject again, even though the disturbances continued right up until the end of the holidays.

I was relieved to return to school where I would be reasonably safe from any paranormal activity, and if anything should happen at school it would be difficult to prove because of the number of boys who could deliberately or accidentally move objects.

During a weekend at home, in the next term, on two or three occasions I was struck lightly from behind by cushions that were being projected from one side of the room to the other.

Several days later my pen disappeared from the desk in my study at school. I thought it must have been stolen or "borrowed" by a schoolfriend. I found it in the study next door, and as all the occupants denied having taken it from my room, I decided that I must have left it in there by mistake, even though I could not remember having been there. It soon disappeared again under similar circumstances, and this time I found it in a different study further away. This process was repeated with other objects as well, although at this stage it was not possible to rule out mischief by my fellow pupils.

Although it appeared impossible to prove that the happenings at school were not caused by "friends" there was an incident which we had to accept as paranormal. Three of us sat in our study together one night, listening to a record. I got up to put another record on the turntable, ready to operate the arm with an automatic switch. As I pushed this switch, the record began to lift off the turntable, revolving in a different direction to the turntable below it, and rising slowly up the centre shaft. When it reached the top of the shaft it stopped, and jammed there, making it difficult to move it without exerting some force.

In April 1971 I went home for the Easter holidays. It soon became evident that the phenomena were increasing in intensity in my room, and, unknown to me at this time, outside it.

A few days after I had returned home my parents had noticed objects that were not in their usual positions; they thought that these things had been moved accidentally or deliberately by a member of the family. These thoughts were dispelled when a torch was found in the middle of the pantry floor when my mother came down to make breakfast; this they had no explanation for. At the time they did not mention it to anybody, so that we were both playing the same game of experiencing paranormal happenings and saying nothing to each other. The pattern of events did not continue for much more than a week when we were all witness to a chaotic holocaust of frighteningly powerful poltergeist phenomena, which was to continue for over three months.

CHAPTER II

On Easter Sunday my parents had some friends in during the evening, and I was out of the house. I came home and shortly afterwards their friends left at about ten o'clock.

As they were showing their guests to the door they passed through the dining room, and to my mother's embarrassment found a large pewter charger upside down on the table; they said nothing to their friends or to me about it.

I had gone to bed by this time and I lay there restlessly although I do not remember whether it was particularly hot that night. I suddenly heard a scraping noise coming from the direction of the cupboard, which continued for about thirty seconds. Having listened to it for a moment, I switched on my lamp and saw to my horror that the cupboard was inching out from the wall towards me. When it halted it had advanced about eighteen inches. I switched off the light and almost simultaneously my bed started to vibrate violently back and forth. I was now too timid to move and I lay in anticipation of whatever might happen next. The vibrating ceased and I felt the end of my bed rising from the floor at the bottom end, to what I estimated to be about one foot. My head end of the bed then rose two or three inches, and at the same time the bed pitched out towards the centre of the room and finally settled at a tangent to the wall.

I was not going to accept being shunted around and I got out of bed as quickly as I could, intent on informing my parents that I had enough, and that I was not going to occupy the room any more until something was done about it.

It transpired that they were not free from worry either; first they had found the pewter charger upturned on the dining room table and then on returning to the sitting room they saw the settee pulled out at an angle across the room. When we went to inspect my bedroom we found a heavy armchair placed across the doorway barring any entry to the room. It was at this stage that for a second time in five years we felt we were caught up in some freakish and frightening dilemma.

I spent that night upstairs in my parents' room on the floor in a sleeping bag, and although we all feared the worst, nothing more occurred until early next morning.

The first room we saw was the dining room. It looked as though a bomb had hit it. Chairs were upturned or simply not in the room, the table was no longer on its feet, and ornaments were strewn around the room and on the floor. The sitting room was in a similar state as was nearly every other ground floor room in the house. Tables and chairs were piled on top of each other, pictures were dismounted and several objects, such as a kettle, and pieces of cutlery, had vanished. Having inspected the field of battle we began to replace everything as it had been previously, starting in the sitting room. We moved to the dining room and corrected the disarrayed furniture; we found an object here that had been moved from the sitting room, and on returning it there, we found that this room was again in a state of total disarray, just minutes after we had tidied it. After the kitchen and dining room had been tidied up we righted the sitting room again. This took us only a few minutes, by which time the dining room had again been "attacked".

This sequence of upsetting one room after another continued all day on Easter Monday, and although we were obviously worried, we could see an amusing side to it all. We were perturbed because we could not understand it, and we did not know what would or could happen next. Objects were constantly being moved, but could never, at this stage, be seen to move.

It was not unusual to find the kettle in the deep-freeze, all the chairs placed on the table, a hat hung up on a nail where a picture should have been, or a broom balanced across the back of a chair.

On the second day of the outbreak, when my brother and sister were entering the kitchen early in the morning, they were met, as they came through the kitchen door, by a trolley which was gliding towards them about an inch from the floor; they turned and ran away and the trolley was found soon afterwards jammed in the doorway where they had been standing. They later watched a detergent bottle rocking from side to side on the edge of the bath, while no one else was near it.

This sequence of events continued in the same fashion for several days. It was soon evident that the phenomena became particularly pronounced at certain times of the day, chiefly mid-morning and evening.

The events that took place were peculiar and even amusing; yet at the same time they were often too difficult to be reproduced by any member of the family. Some of the most interesting demonstrations were those that involved delicate balancing feats, and on more than one occasion we found a broom balanced across the horizontal handrail of our staircase. It was easily off-balanced from its position when touched. In our sitting room we had three metal framed tables with stone tops, and these were occasionally delicately placed one on top of the other; the total weight of the tables was obviously great. Beds seemed to suffer more than any other pieces of furniture, and they were frequently stripped completely, or even overturned. My sister's bed was particularly "victimised", and on one occasion it was found with two of its feet hanging out of a first floor window. Many objects disappeared, to be found later hidden or returned to a different, and usually very obvious place. These were not necessarily small articles, but also included pictures, bed clothes, kitchen equipment and ornaments which would often be found in the backs of cupboards or under beds.

My father was worried and keen to see an end to these activities; he tried to seek advice from Dr. George Owen, only to find that he had recently emigrated to Canada. This increased the dilemma, because there was now nothing we could do except watch as this assertive force tried to dominate us and rule the house. We were again faced with the problem of having no one to turn to.

Further, we were surprised and intimidated by an uncanny ability of the poltergeist to carry out almost anything that anyone happened to suggest, including the turning-on of lights and taps. It had, so it seemed, an affinity for electrical appliances. During the first days of the phenomenon, an electric ring on our cooker blew out, rendering it cracked and unusable, and causing a fuse in the main fuse box to blow so that the ceramic fuse case was filled with the molten metal of the destroyed fuse. Light bulbs seemed to have a shortened life span, and the cooker adopted a peculiar habit of turning itself on, unless it was unplugged.

Child-like scribbles materialized on walls throughout the house; these were usually executed with the lead from a pencil. Although they looked as if they were drawn with a pencil, they were in fact seen to grow on the wall, from the centre outwards, without any pencil being used. They were like a spreading cancer; scribbly "circles" such as a young child would accomplish. About fifteen of these appeared, until they were superseded by a similarly implemented scrawl, akin to an astrological Leo sign (my birthday is in August). These "designs" were about two or three inches in diameter. The scribbling that followed later was somewhat more worrying, or at least, it was to me. On more than one occasion I saw on the walls the words, "Matthew Beware", in a child-like handwriting. The warnings did not tell me what to beware of, and I ignored them as much as possible. It was as though there was a child causing many of the disturbances, because so many of the occurrences displayed a childish mentality.

After we had become more or less accustomed to the movements of objects, we were subjected to a new spectacle which was equally much of a nuisance. This was the covering of areas of floor with water which we found to be coming from the "U" bends of wash basins and lavatory bowls in the house. The water, having been in some way removed, would be discovered in large pools on the floor; this phenomenon did seem to limit itself to one area of stone floor in the hall, with one or two exceptions.

It then stopped using just water and would use whatever liquid happened to be in the house. On other occasions we found acid, paint-strippers, and ink poured on the floor, all of which could be traced to containers in the house. One example is particularly interesting: we found a liquid poured all over a linoleum covered floor upstairs. This had dissolved the floor covering and seeped underneath it to the wooden floor boards. It later dissolved cloths that were used to mop it up, and it burned the skin. We decided that it was sodium hydroxide, as there was in the cellar a jar of sodium hydroxide crystals, which had been used for cleaning an old dirty sink. These crystals had found their way into the water on the floor upstairs.

Sometimes all the drawers and cupboard doors in the kitchen would be found hanging open, or a vase of flowers, or an ornament might be discovered in the oven. I remember on one occasion starting to lay the table for lunch; I had placed the mats around the table and I went to fetch the cutlery which was already on a tray in the kitchen. This could not have taken me more than twenty seconds, but by the time I returned, the mats were no longer on the table. They were found laid out on the floor in the sitting room, in exactly the same positions they had been in on the table.

After the poltergeist activities had been going on for two weeks, it became clear that a certain pattern was emerging. The phenomenon was basically divisible into three categories: the first was purely disruptive and annoying, the second was concerned with symmetry and balance, and the third was a demonstration of noisy and boisterous movement, designed it seemed, to attract spectators.

I have already described the first category, which was chiefly movement of furniture and domestic disruption; the second category included the balancing tricks, and events such as the table mats. The third type was probably the most interesting, as we could actually witness the happening in progress. Objects would be hurled up the stairs, with great force and noise, from the bottom and could be watched in flight if one stood at the top of the stairs. Often I could sit in the dining room and watch as objects passed me by, flying through the room and up the stairs. Occasionally these articles came from the dining room where I sat but usually appeared from the kitchen. They would first vibrate, then shake violently until they rose up into the air to move away. Bends or obstacles presented no hindrance and were carefully negotiated. The objects once in flight, gained speed as they approached the stairs until they struck a wall, falling onto the stairs with great noise. Particularly heavy items caused a lot of commotion when they crashed, such as hammers, mallets, wooden coat-hangers, blocks of wood, gallon cans of paint-stripper and carpentery tools. Those who watched these objects from the landing on the first floor noted that they were capable of turning the two right-angles on the staircase, and sometimes lobbing themselves over the handrail at the top of the stairs, onto the landing. This always happened either during the middle of the morning, or early in the evening.

My sister had in her bedroom a table about twenty-nine inches high by thirty-six inches long by eighteen inches wide; it also held a drawer under the top of it. Her bedroom was at the front of the house, on the first floor. On the table she kept a pile of books and papers, a mug of pencils and other ornaments.

This table with everything on it vanished one afternoon. We searched the house for it, but in vain. On a second search a little later, it was discovered standing in our cellar, with all the papers and ornaments still exactly in place on it. In fact it appeared that none of the objects on it had been disturbed. It had travelled no less than 105 feet, descended three flights of stairs, passed through five doorways, some of less than 30 inches wide, and made no less than ten complete right-angled changes of direction.

Another startling incident that really amounted to a show of force occurred when a heavy double-bed with all its coverings was up-ended. The total force required to carry out such a feat is immense. Let it suffice to state that my father and I could just about lift it back *down* onto the floor.

One afternoon another warning appeared on the wall, "Matthew Beware". It was scrawled, as usual, in a child-like hand in pencil. I cannot recollect what prompted the suggestion, but my mother ventured that I might place a piece of paper on the dining room table for this writing to appear on. This seemed quite a good idea, if for nothing else than to see if the poltergeist was capable of using it. All the curtains were drawn because we had noticed that the poltergeist appeared to work better if it was not likely to be watched, and we left a pencil and a sheet of paper on the table. My mother and I left the room and went upstairs, leaving the dining room locked with the latches closed; no one else was in the house. When we returned ten minutes later the paper had a typical scrawl scribbled on it. On another sheet I wrote across the top the alphabet and numbers 0 to 9, which I left on the table as before. The procedure was repeated, and when we came back a quarter of an hour later, several small scribblings were dotted around the paper, together with another Leo sign. In the middle appeared the words "Matthew Beware". Although we did not recognise it at the time, this was a very significant move, because it proved that I really was the source of the energy supplying the poltergeist; more important still, it was a first step towards controlling the poltergeist. Actual control was not achieved, however, for some months.

It was about this time that another significant facet of the phenomenon became obvious. I was at home with my mother and we were both upstairs when she asked me to move a small wicker basket from kitchen table onto the dining room table.

Fifteen minutes later when we both came downstairs, the basket had been carefully placed in the middle of the dining room table as requested.

It was nearing the end of the holidays and I was about to return to school. On the day before I was due to leave there were still several objects that having disappeared, had not been found, and my parents were anxious to have them returned before I left. They asked me therefore to try and get these objects returned; they were mainly small things such as teaspoons or crockery. While we were all in our dining room I agreed to try and get these articles returned to a table in the sitting room.

We were amazed at the selection of domestic items that we found placed on the table half an hour later. We were quite ignorant of the number of objects that had in fact disappeared. I was even more surprised that they had been returned. Table mats, cutlery, books and ornaments were found on the table in the sitting room and most of the objects had not been noted as missing.

It was decided by my father that he would go and talk to the Headmaster and put him fully in the picture.

CHAPTER III

"From what Mr. Manning wrote, I gather", wrote Dr. George Owen to the Headmaster shortly afterwards, "that you coped with the situation with great sympathy and judgment. It is very difficult in any institution with responsibility for general order, morale, and conduct of normal business to suffer a disturbance but I am sure your decision to keep Matthew at the school, besides being very humane, was entirely justified. I am hoping very much that you can struggle through with the situation until the end of term. If any suggestions of mine are in order, I would recommend for the sake of the boys, attempting to dispel any idea that the happenings are "supernatural" in the sense of angelic or demonic intervention, spirits of the dead, etc."

The Headmaster was due for a long term during which time he began to despair on two occasions, trying to understand something which he had never encountered before. He was taking a great risk in allowing me to stay, being responsible as he was, for so many boys. He was my Housemaster as well as being Headmaster.

On the evening of my return I was summoned by a rather worried and apprehensive Headmaster to his study. He admitted that he had never come into contact with anything of this nature before, and that he had no idea of how to remedy the situation. However, he was quite prepared to follow any suggestions that anyone might have, if they would bring about a speedy termination of the phenomenon. As it happened, we were fortunate to have as Matron in the house, a woman who possessed the gift of E.S.P. She suggested someone whom she thought could be of help. Matron had arrived about four weeks before the end of the last term, and I had not met her before.

The news "that something was up" had gone round my circle of friends rather quickly. I cannot remember what their reactions were at the time. However, during my first night at school in the dormitory, nothing happened. The next day too was uneventful, much to my surprise, because it was the first time that nothing had occurred for some weeks.

In the dormitory I had been allocated the bottom bed of a bunk, with no occupant above me. There were twenty-six boarders occupying the dormitory, which was square in shape, with a large square ground to ceiling cupboard in the middle. All of us were in the fifth form, due to take our "O" levels that term. My bunk was in the corner of the dormitory, by a window, and away from the other beds.

It did not stay away from the other beds for very long. On my second night back at school it shifted itself out from the wall soon after the lights had been switched off. I got out of bed and pushed it eighteen inches back into the corner. Within two minutes it was moving again, much to the amazement of several other boys who could see it from where they lay. This time I did not return it to its proper place, but let it stay where it was, about eighteen inches away from both walls; shortly afterwards an empty bunk next to where mine had been, began to move sideways towards another block of beds. This bunk stopped after about six feet leaving an empty area near my bed, which was soon filled by my bunk which shunted about four feet in the same direction as the other one. This caused a great commotion among the occupants of the dormitory, and the lights were switched on. The disturbed beds were returned to where they belonged and with much chattering the lights were extinguished. When my bed moved out again I left it where it was, and slept with it out of place for that night.

Surprisingly enough, the events of the night were only discussed within the circle of the occupants of the dormitory, which meant that only those people knew anything about the moving beds, except, of course, the Headmaster and the Matron who had been told by a friend of mine. Nobody talked openly about the beds for some weeks, because the other dormitory incumbents were frightened of being made to look stupid by anyone who had not actually experienced these events.

The same occurrences took place on the following night, with much the same reaction from everybody in the dormitory; some of them were quite unnerved by the fact that the bunks were difficult to move, let alone with somebody inside. The bunks had heavy metal frames, the feet being tipped with rubber buffers and without castors.

Nothing occurred during day time on the first two days as far as I know.

After a third night of upheaval in the dormitory, a friend of mine went to see the Matron. The Headmaster had decided to let events run as they happened, because there was not very much disturbance

Although Matron was indirectly instrumental in the eventual control of the phenomenon, she really became far too involved and adopted a very subjective attitude which led to an entirely uncritical

After violent outbreaks of poltergeist phenomena during Matthew's Easter holidays in 1971, his father's fears that such phenomena might occur at the boarding school as well were found to be justified. For three years, until Matthew left school in 1973, not only Matthew but most members of his school house were witnesses to extraordinary happenings. Three times the Headmaster asked Matthew's parents to take Matthew away from school; but each time he relented. Throughout his stay at school, Matthew (1) had the support of the Matron (2). At her suggestion, the Headmaster consulted "outsiders" for help, and the House Tutor (3) accompanied Matthew to a strange meeting where an expert instructed the young man in the use of banishing rituals and exorcism.

43

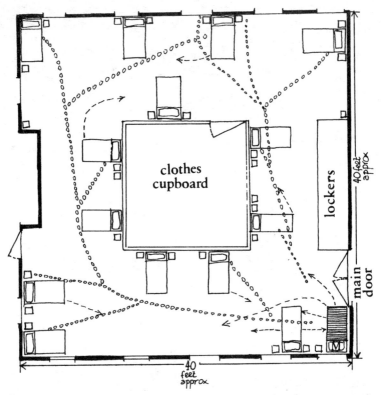

□ – – – – – – – chair
– – – – ▶ – – – – movement of beds
○○○○○○ – – – – course of poltergeist propelled apports
M – – – – – – – – Matthew's bed
all beds were the two tier bunk type

clothes
cupboard

lockers

main
door

40 feet
approx

40
feet
approx

The happenings which took place in the boy's dormitory caused the most serious upheavals. Heavy steel double-bunk beds moved of their own accord. Apports materialised and were propelled with force around the room. On one occasion fourteen table knives were "thrown" against walls and beds. The origin of the knives, which bore a royal crest and the initials GR, could not be established. Other apports, such as broken glass, nails and pebbles made sleeping in the dormitory almost impossible. It was mainly these happenings which caused serious unrest among the parents of other pupils.

Other dormitories were also disturbed; glowing lights would appear on walls and the heat emanating from the light spots threatened to set the whole house on fire. The poltergeist phenomena lessened in intensity and finally stopped when Matthew allowed himself to be "used" for automatic writing.

acceptance. She was a person who genuinely wanted to help, but unfortunately she had a habit of getting the wrong end of the stick and then airing her views. Matron was one of those ladies who try to get into contact with "the other side" in darkened rooms. She asked my friend to tell me to come and see her; perhaps she could help the spirit.

I spoke with her for over two hours and she felt sure she could help; although she too had never come across anything quite like this before.

The next night, as if to make up for lost day time, we were subjected to more phenomena and poltergeist displays in the dormitory. Not only did my bunk move as it had done on the previous three nights, but two other bunks as well, much to the surprise of their occupants. It soon became apparent that objects were being thrown around the room, and when the lights were switched on, the floor was found to be covered in pieces of broken glass, screws and nails. We got a broom and quickly swept the glass and the other objects into a heap in a corner. When the lights were put out, they again flew to all corners of the room. This continued for about an hour, and seemed to die down as people went off to sleep.

This the Headmaster found rather more worrying, especially when it was discovered early next morning that my study had been deranged during that night. What was he to say if parents of boys 'phoned him up and demanded an explanation? Reports of what had happened were bound to get back to them. They were sure to accuse him of allowing schoolboy pranks to interfere with their sons' sleep in their "O" level term. He was therefore very keen to see a hasty conclusion to these events.

During the following night, Thursday, the same things happened again, and various apports were hurled around the dormitory. These included broken glass, pebbles, cutlery and pieces of wood, which were thrown apparently with great force towards a wall or a window, where they would cause much noise. It was quite clear that none of the boys caused this mischief, because the dormitory, being without curtains, was at this time of year still fairly light at about ten o'clock. Anyone throwing these objects would have quickly been seen by someone. Naturally everybody, although timidly, was on the look out for anyone who might be throwing these objects.

It was evident the next day that the disturbances had spread to the studies of other dormitory occupants. The studies were in a seperate block, away from other buildings, and were used during the daytime for work and leisure. Pools of water appeared on large areas of the floors, and bookcases were emptied or upturned, as were other pieces of furniture.

The Headmaster was taking no more chances and he followed up the name of a gentleman which the Matron had given him. He had knowledge of the subject, and Matron suggested that he could help. The Headmaster spoke to him over the telephone, only to be told that he could not himself help, instead the Headmaster was given another address. A further telephone call was made and the Headmaster was told that I could see somebody on the following Saturday, which was just over a week ahead. Obviously this was better than nothing, even though we had to witness these occurrences for another week. This was not very comforting to the Headmaster, who decided to call in the school chaplain to see if he could be of assistance.

After a short discussion with me the chaplain decided that such psychic phenomena were outside his scope and that although he had heard of similar cases, there was nothing he could do to ease the situation. The phenomenon in the dormitory was very much akin to the staircase displays that had occurred at my home. On many occasions when we were all in bed, objects would hurtle towards somebody, as if to strike the person, and then either swing away at an angle, just before he was hit or strike him so lightly that it was hardly felt. Hurling objects missed people literally by a few inches and often hit the wall behind their head.

One event that made a lasting impression in more than one way, was when an apport, in the shape of a four ounce brass weight, hurtled from one end of the dormitory to the other, striking the metal frame of a bunk with a resounding crack. It made such a noise that the lights were switched on; it was found that the frame had been dented by the weight, which gives some indication of the force behind these objects. Had it veered a fraction of a degree in either direction it would have hit somebody. The Headmaster's worries grew daily.

Objects, none of which belonged in the dormitory, would be thrown and it was soon noted that certain missiles would appear one night and not the next. One night nothing but glass would materialise, and on the following night it would be only nails. Other apports included skewers, stones, pieces of broken concrete, and spoons. Terror struck the dormitory when on one night bone-handled knives were thrown, which no one had seen before. By the next morning fourteen of these knives were picked up from the floor. Several of these had struck people very gently, and one or two of them narrowly missed fellow pupils as they hurtled towards the walls.

46

On the Thursday of that week I received in the post an unexpected letter from the Reverend Dr. E. K. L. Quine (Honorary Canon of Leicester Cathedral), "Dear Matthew," it said, "I received a telephone call today from the mother of David, who has apparently been concerned about you, and this in itself is worth noting in a day and age when people tend more and more to look after themselves. Both David and his mother want to help and yet quite understandably did not know how to begin. His mother spoke to me because I am the Bishop's representative on the Churches Fellowship for Psychical and Spiritual Studies and I do know a little about these things.

"If you want my help I will give it to you.

"Meanwhile do not be too worried. There is an explanation for these things and the matter can be dealt with satisfactorily.

". . . Bless you now. It will come right if handled properly."

I decided not to reply to the letter until after I had seen the person in Leicester whom I was to meet on the Saturday.

On Thursday night we were subjected to the now usual poltergeist displays in the dormitory, and that night it chose metal coathangers to hurl around. The next morning nearly twenty of these were found on the floor. Many of them had been completely squashed so that they were little more than balls of heavy gauge wire. The activity now continued through the day, and seemed to occur within a certain radius of wherever I settled. During the daytime studies were disturbed in as many ways as seemed possible.

Friday night it was broken glass again, which as usual began flying about at ten o'clock when the lights were put out. Also during that night the wooden chairs beside the beds took to dancing and capered round the dormitory, colliding with anything that happened to be in the way.

In our dormitory were boys of the same age as myself, and directly underneath was another dormitory similar to ours, occupied by boys one or two years younger than ourselves. They would lie in their beds and listen to the commotion above them, with little knowledge of what was happening.

At 4.30 on Saturday morning a prefect in a smaller dormitory in another part of the house had an interesting experience, which was the start of a different form of phenomenon. Why it happened to him I cannot explain, except that at the time we were close friends. He awoke at that time for no apparent reason and noticed how icy cold it was where he lay. On the wall opposite him he saw a disc of luminous light. It was, he said, about eighteen inches in diameter and initially he thought it was a light being projected under the door, from a source in the corridor outside. The coldness intensified and as it did so the size of the patch of light increased. It continued to grow until it was some three feet in diameter and by now my friend was becoming increasingly frightened. After it had spread from the skirting board to the ceiling and was about six feet across he left his bed and prayed in the corridor outside. After he had been praying for about half an hour he was found by the Matron; the light had almost disappeared when they returned to the dormitory. I was told of this incident later that morning, and this event heralded a change in course of the phenomena, as they were, and I believe this was the first occasion where actual spirit intervention occurred.

It could have been said that the objects in the dormitory were thrown by the occupants themselves and were not caused by a poltergeist at all. On one occasion one of the boys began throwing objects from the other side of the dormitory and was immediately seen by others, whereupon he stopped. Afterwards he was so badly plagued for several days by phenomena that he had to be treated with tranquillizers; he eventually left the house at the request of the Headmaster. He claimed that I was the root of his problems, and that he had thrown the objects himself in the hope of getting me removed from the school which would end his troubles. This was the most extreme example of the effect that these experiences had on people at school. Most of them learned to live with the happenings and accept them; some were frightened, some were frightened of me, others were sceptical and suspicious. In the last category were those who had not been directly involved and who had not seen anything themselves; they were pupils in other houses. It was interesting to note how the witnesses to the occurrences vehemently supported their validity even at the risk of being ridiculed. The overall effect of the happenings was to provide a strong sense of "fellow feeling", as someone put it; we became very tightly knit. To a very large extent the saying that "to see is to believe" was true amongst those who had experienced the poltergeist for themselves.

On Saturday afternoon, 8th May, I was taken to see a gentleman in a nearby town, who, I had been told, could be of help. I was rather doubtful. The House Tutor took me to a large mental hospital where this man worked, and right from the start I sensed that there was something strange about him. I did not trust him and found him not to be frank. There was little doubt, however, that he was a psychic. I do not know exactly what post he held within the hospital; we were shown into a small room, where he sat with a dark-haired woman.

I had taken with me a basket full of apports that had been found in the dormitory, but he was not interested. Out of a small book he produced a ritual which he claimed would rid me of the trouble, and asked me to copy it down:

"Face east. Touch forehead and say ATEH (thou art). Touch breast and say MALKUTH (the Kingdom). Touch right shoulder and say VE-GEBURAH (and the Power). Touch left shoulder and say VE-GEDULAH (and the Glory). Clasp hands before you and say LE-OLAM (forever). Point up and say AMEN. Make in the air toward the East the banishing Pentagram, vibrate the deity name— YOD HE VAU HE. Imagine your voice carries forward to the East of the Universe. Hold out finger before you, go to South, make the Pentagram and vibrate similarly the deity name ADONAI. Go to West,, make Pentagram and vibrate EHEIEH. Go to North, make the Pentagram and vibrate AGLA. Return to East and complete your circle by bringing the finger point to centre of the first Pentagram. Stand with arms outstretched in the form of a cross and say—Before me Raphael (Air), Behind me Gabriel (Water), at my right hand Michael (Fire), at my left hand Auriel (Earth). Before me flames the Pentagram, behind me shines the six-rayed star. Make again the Quabalistic Cross as directed above saying ATEH, etc . . ."

This I was instructed to do every time something paranormal occurred. I thought this was a ridiculous suggestion, because I should be doing this all day. I took the ritual with an air of scepticism and said nothing. Could it really bring an end to these occurrences? For the next one and a half hours the tutor and myself were subjected to an extraordinary display of clairvoyance, by both the man and the woman. We were given an analysis of our characters and lives, which, whether we cared to admit it or not, was correct and quite impressive. We were also told of similar experiences of other people which were interesting, and much was said of various occult circles. I was then strongly warned to have nothing to do with Black Magic. Although I had no intentions of dabbling in such matters, it was not until sometime later that I realised how hypocritical these words had been, and how my tutor and I nearly got trapped in such practices by the very same person who had warned me. One of the other subjects he mentioned was astral projection. He explained to us how it was done and spoke of his experiences in the field. When we left the hospital we both had come to the conclusion that we should never have been sent there in the first place. Today I am convinced that the man practiced magic and was highly unsuitable to give advice to me.

As soon as I returned to school that evening I went up to the dormitory by myself and performed the banishing ritual. I had been told that if I drew the pentagrams the wrong way the same procedure would work as an invoking force which could be most dangerous. Within two hours it looked as if I might have repeated the banishing ritual in reverse, as havoc was ensuing. I repeated it twice more in the dormitory before it became obvious that we would only get peace if I left the room. I did not therefore go to bed that night, and from that time onwards, I believe that the poltergeist activity actually began to wane.

Before the other dormitory occupants went to bed that night, the Matron gathered them in the ground floor washing room and talked to them about what she knew of the subject, which I was told was rather garbled, but reassuring in the situation; she did act at that time as an emotional defuser, which was what was required. While she was thus engaged I was in the Headmaster's study informing him of what had happened. He was by this time very worried as several parents had already telephoned him asking for an explanation. His predicament was not easy: he had to give some explanation to the parents, and he felt that he would have to ask me to leave the school if he received further calls. What explanation was he going to offer to the governors or trustees of the school for removing me? He would look quite foolish if he said that I was the centre of a poltergeist outbreak. If I did have to go he might have to face inquiries from the Press which would have given the school a bad reputation. He felt he was faced with a dilemma.

During the gathering with the Matron, inexplicable phenomena occurred in front of the whole assembly, about thirty people. While they were standing in one large group, listening to what Matron said, a plug was thrown from an empty corner of the room, landing at the Matron's feet, very much to her delight! This was followed by several pieces of broken glass which appeared to fall from the ceiling. The startled group retired to bed with plenty to talk about, and I prepared to stay up the rest of the night with the Matron in her sitting room. I had a very strong feeling that much was going to take place during the night and that it was probably just as well that I was not going to bed; at least the rest of the dormitory would have a peaceful night without me in the room.

We talked in Matron's room with some other boys who went off to bed at about eleven-thirty. After they had gone and we were on our own, chippings of wood and small pebbles and pieces of glass appeared in the room. They materialised on our laps and fell into cups of coffee; all the while there seemed to be an unusual amount of noise, knockings and raps from the walls, floor and ceiling, as well as the characteristic pinging sounds which came from the windows, pictures, and even cups.

At about midnight when most pupils were asleep, the Matron went around all the dormitories to check that everything was in order and that there was no disturbance: everything was quiet.

Just over an hour later, when everything was still and quiet except for the wall rappings in Matron's room, an icy chill swirled around our feet and the lower part of our legs. It was a sensation I have felt many times since then. It is like having ether poured over one's leg. It crept gradually up until it was so bad that we were both forced to move. When we did so we lost this sensation: it was as if it was only surrounding the immediate area we had occupied. We both suspected that this "freezing" effect heralded something that was about to happen and we left the room and entered a small junior dormitory next to Matron's sitting room. This was occupied by eight young boys with two older prefects in charge.

The same ether-like cold appeared to creep into this room, and on the wall opposite the door was a small patch of light. There was no light in the passage that the dormitory door opened into. Putting my hand up in front of this patch of light, no shadow could be seen, as if the light was being emitted from the wall, rather than projected or reflected onto it. When I felt this patch on the wall, it was very warm, unlike the surrounding area which was as cool as an uncovered plaster wall usually is. We stood back from it, waiting for it to grow as it had when it was seen previously; it did.

"We stood, Matthew and I, staring at this apparition on the wall opposite to the door, above the head of a sleeping boy. It was a small round bright light which gradually grew larger. Suddenly Chris woke; the cold had penetrated through his sleep, and he too saw this bright lighted circle on the wall," the Matron wrote down afterwards, and she continued: "I quietly said, 'It's all right, Matthew, I can see a cross placed centrally across it'. Matthew said, It's a crown of thorns round the edge'. We had no lights on—the light of this apparition was bright enough to illuminate the dormitory."

This is how Matron described what she saw, and is particularly interesting because what she saw and what I saw was not the same. I saw the patch of light surrounded by what looked like a band or crown of thorns, whilst the Matron did not see this—she saw a cross over the light, which I could not see.

Once again I faced East and repeated the banishing ritual, concentrating on removing the light from the wall. After twenty minutes

51

it began to shrink until it was a saucer-sized area without the cross or the thorns. We then switched on the electric light and the para-normal light disappeared completely.

With the waning of the light on the wall the temperature began to rise again until it felt more like normal room temperature. We stayed in the dormitory for some minutes after this, until we were satisfied that there was no further disturbance.

During the remainder of the night very little happened other than the usual manifestations, such as the tossing of pebbles about the room or the rapping noises. The dormitories remained quiet and still until the following morning when life resumed again as normal.

Early on Sunday morning the Headmaster decided that he could no longer keep me in the school while this phenomenon was going on. He had put up with about four weeks of these disturbances with great patience. Accordingly he telephoned my parents who agreed to have a meeting with him that afternoon. To me it was some kind of relief, in so much as I would no longer be disturbing the other members of the House, and we all had "O" level examinations quickly approaching.

I was still in the Matron's sitting room when he made his decision. Shortly afterwards a strange thing happened, as we sat together discussing the Headmaster's decision, which Matron considered most unjust. She had made up her mind that she would go and talk to him and try to persuade him to change his mind. There was a knock on the door and a prefect, who had been inspecting the dormitories came in. He gave something to her that he had found near my bed. It was a length of wire, twisted into a saucer-sized ring, and a grey soft-covered booklet. On the cover was a crucifix with a crown of thorns placed centrally over it; on opening it we found it to be a copy of "The Saint John and Saint Matthew Passion". Apart from the two names, Matthew, my own, and John, the Headmaster's, it was more than a coincidence, since the design on the cover was the same as I had seen on the wall during the night.

By mid-morning the Headmaster had reversed his decision with regard to my leaving school, and when my parents arrived the situation was relatively normal. My father spoke with him for some time, and it was agreed that I could stay, as the Headmaster thought the happenings were on the decline.

While my parents were still at the school a telephone call was received from the man at the mental hospital, and he spoke to the Matron. Not only did he claim to have invoked the light on the wall, but also to have projected himself astrally into the room we were in, where he claimed to have seen me and the Matron. If continued to carry out the banishing ritual, he said, the poltergeist manifestations would give way to a controlled use of the psycho-kinetic energy, or words to that effect.

In an anxious state, my parents left without me and returned home. Their main concern was the psychological effect this experi-ence was having on me and the other pupils.

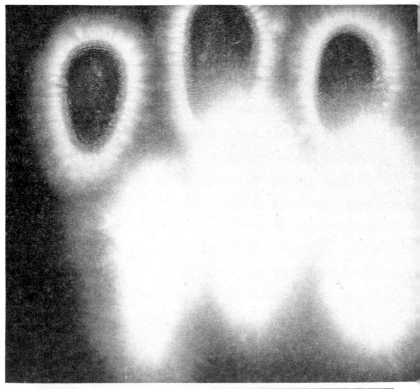

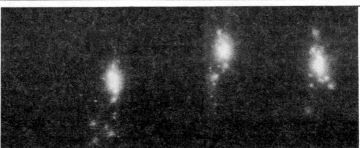

Prof. Douglas Dean, one of the leading authorities on Kirlian Photography, carried out a series of experiments with Matthew. He afterwards stated, "The results we have received are absolutely unique! I have never seen anything like this before." On 23 June 1974 a series of Kirlian photos were taken of Matthew's fingertips. The top impressions (control) shows Matthew's normal radiation (1). This is already stronger than that of most people. The second set of fingerprints (2) shows his radiation when he deliberately "switched his power on". This experiment, however, yielded an unexpected bonus in that the radiation had shown up on the print beneath. Matthew was then asked to focus the energy to pinpoints; this he did (3).

CHAPTER IV

SHORTLY afterwards the Headmaster received a letter from Dr. George Owen, who wrote:

"I investigated a minor outbreak of poltergeist phenomena at Mr. Manning's home a few years back. I believed that they were not due to trickery, but real phenomena. The evidence did not allow them being ascribed to Matthew in particular as the involuntary source. The probabilities were that they would not recur. This latter guess has been proved wrong.

"It may be helpful, however, to record my opinions on the present events as recorded by Mr. Manning.

"(1) I am sure the events are genuine phenomena without any trickery or bad faith on Matthew's part.

"(2) Even though he is achieving some measure of voluntary control, the original phenomena were totally involuntary and no possible blame should attach to him for the earlier ones. Similarly it would be wrong to suppose that he can control everything that happens now.

"(3) There would be no justification for supposing without either *very* expert and highly *specific* evidence to the contrary that Matthew is psychologically abnormal or disturbed, except insofar as the occurrences themselves might disturb anyone. The powers he is exhibiting are rare and unusual, but there is no reason to believe that they are the result of emotional ill-health.

"I think a brief address to the School, or the House, or the forms most concerned would be useful in 'lowering the temperature', e.g. These events, though rare, do occur more often than is supposed. They are not due to tricks, or people "seeing things". They are due to unusual physical forces which people sometimes develop without being aware of. These forces are the subject of active study by scientists in England, U.S.A., Canada and Europe. The best authorities believe them to be natural though rare. They are not supernatural. This particular case is one of a kind that happens somewhere in the world every few months. Others are doubtless going on elsewhere. Many people have rare talents, e.g. hearing other people's thoughts. Others have the ability to move objects by the unknown force. When talents start up like this it is scientifically extremely important and interesting. The scientific interest outweighs the minor inconveniences the events occasion. This is a very good opportunity to observe all these things in a detached and scientific way."

"I have always found, even with very excited or frightened people that this cool scientific approach is very effective in 'emotional defusing'."

The Headmaster did not take Dr. Owen's advice; he never addressed the School or spoke openly about what was happening. It was only too obvious that something was going on, but he always insisted on never mentioning the whole affair and acting as if it did not exist. This had the effect of causing widespread rumours later and much was said that was completely fictitious.

The following Monday morning, I deliberately added a new dimension to the phenomenon. As I had no lessons, I decided to find out if I could astrally project myself home, since if I succeeded, what I saw could be verified. Following as closely as possible the instructions that I had been given on Saturday afternoon, I attempted to leave my body. Although I can remember exactly what I did, I don't know whether I achieved astral projection.

Lying on the bed it seemed more like day-dreaming. I remember one moment being "above" myself, so that I could quite clearly see my body on the bed. Thinking and concentrating on home, the next thing I saw was the back of our house, with the doors and windows opened, as they usually are in warm weather. Going inside, through the open back door, I saw my mother at the kitchen sink with the washing machine by her. She turned round and looked towards where I was standing; then after a few moments she went back to her job. I could see quite clearly although everything was strangely quiet. Shortly afterwards my mother went to the dining room and I followed her. She looked round again to the spot where I was and I felt that she was looking at me. This went on for about ten to twenty minutes. As she wandered around the house, it seemed that she was looking for me; she persistently looked in my direction although obviously she did not actually see me.

I later questioned her about this occasion, and we exchanged both sides of our experience. She had not seen me, but she had "felt" that I was in the house on that morning; she had the feeling that I was standing behind her, watching her while she was in the kitchen. She had walked round the house looking for me, and was half expecting to see me. I had a headache for several days after this experience.

The poltergeist phenomena continued and appeared to be unchecked as yet, despite the fact that I was carrying out the banishing ritual as directed. Matron had by now accepted the poltergeist phenomena as normal occurrences. She wrote about them quite casually:

"Beds are found to have moved: heavy iron double bunks that are very hard to move without considerable physical effort and noise. The legs have rubber tips to the legs, not castors. Boys sleeping in them have woken up in the morning to find their beds moved. Often in Matthew's presence I feel this awful cold air, rather as if I had been bathed in ether. In the dormitory, after lights out, nails hurl through the air. Knives come through the air at great velocity and with great force, as does glass, broken porcelain, plates and cutlery. Spoons appeared one night, as had knives, and I could not identify them, except that the spoons bore the crest G.R. and the crown; the knives had in some cases yellowed aged bone handles . . . Never once has any of the missiles hit anyone or hurt them—they seem on contact to bounce off again. One day, cleaning the dormitory, the cleaner found her way out of the dormitory hampered by chairs placed across the doorway as if to stop her leaving.

"Elsewhere in the house, plugs will fly through the air; pools of water appear and light bulbs fall out of their sockets although they rarely break. No structural damage has been caused, but there is always a mess to clear up.

"In my sitting room I might be sitting quietly perhaps sewing, sometimes listening to the wireless, when I am suddenly soaked with coldness, and a shower of pebbles falls from the ceiling. Some nights it may be little chippings of wood which drop into my lap.

"Several times I have come into my room to find perhaps a cushion on the floor, or a chair upturned. Objects are moved, but nothing broken. In fact I am so used to it that after a while it just makes me smile."

A school-friend made the following entry in his diary:
"The time would have been about 10.20 p.m. Since lights out all had been quiet, save the odd screw or nail being projected. A boy in the next bed and myself had been humming tunes, and Richard on becoming irate had got out of bed to hit the other boy and tell him to be quiet. Richard was in a nervous state himself I believe. However, as he stood by our beds a plate crashed to the ground. Obviously it fell from a height of more than a few inches. In fact the noise it made indicated that it fell from at least five or six feet. Strangely enough the plate did not break but landed on the lino floor as a coin often lands, so that it revolved shallowly around

its circumference causing a rolling sound. Everyone was very shocked for a few seconds. (In fact, Richard had leapt onto the nearest bed!) Then suddenly the chatter exploded as can be expected. Five minutes later the second occurrence took place. The noise of the chatter had subsided when an almighty crash was heard again between my bed and Matthew's bed, where the previous incident had taken place. On this occasion either the plate was dropped from a greater height than before, or it was thrown with a larger force, for the result was a shattered plate whose pieces were scattered over an exceptionally wide area . . . some pieces were in fact retrieved as far as ten or twelve feet from the incident."

One night I was woken up by a prefect in the early hours, and asked to go to the small junior dormitory, because they were having trouble there. When I arrived the room was darkened and several people were in there, mostly prefects and boys who had woken up. The room was exceptionally cold and there on the wall was a pool of very bright light, which on touching was too hot for me to keep my hand on. After clearing out all the people who seemed just to be standing around, I carried out the banishing ritual; the Matron came in and again claimed that she could see a cross placed over it. The light did not diminish after I completed the ritual. Another small junior dormitory adjoined the one we were in, and we went into it, to see if anything was happening in there. Nothing could be seen immediately; the Matron put her hand up against the area of wall that backed where the patch of light was manifesting in the other dormitory. She found it to be warm, as I did, and we found it becoming warmer, indicating that the heat was spreading through the wall. Back in the other room I again carried out the banishing ritual in the hope of ridding the wall of the light. Again it failed, and the area had by now become so heated that I switched on the main light, fearing that if some action were not soon taken, the wall could begin to smoulder or burn. It was as though a magnifying glass was being used to focus the sun's rays on to the wall, except that the light appeared to emanate from within the wall. When I carried out the banishing ritual with the light switched on, the manifestation diminished and disappeared.

This episode was duly reported to the Headmaster, for whom it proved yet again to be the last straw. He could not accept the responsibility of a fire, and the events were again preying on his sense of justice, especially when worried parents telephoned later for an explanation. Once more he decided that the only solution "for the benefit of the other members of the House" was to send me home for as long as these events persisted. My parents were summoned on the Sunday.

With persuasion from the Matron, the Headmaster had by Sunday again agreed to allow me to remain in the school.

A week later I returned home for the weekend and during that time another significant turn in the story took place. This was, I believe, the first occasion that I entered into direct communication with spirit entities, and I recorded my experience on paper as soon as it was over.

If, I reasoned, I could travel by astrally projecting myself, why could I not astrally project myself into the past? I thought it even more likely to succeed as I would be carrying out this experiment in our house which had been built in stages between 1550 and 1730.

The state that I lapsed into was really like a trance, and perhaps astral projection is not the correct terminology. I cannot explain how I entered this trance; I seemed to just fall into it naturally, as one might fall asleep.

After what must have been about half an hour, I could hear a woman's soft voice somewhere near my head. I had planned out quite carefully before hand the questions I would ask if I succeeded with the experiment. I had been told by the man in Leicester that if ever I carried out any communication with spirits, to ask them before all else, if they came in peace. I did so and a faint voice replied, "Yes", to my surprise.

"What is your name?" I asked.

"Henrietta.—Henrietta Webb."

"When were you born?"

"In the year of Our dear Lord, sixteen hundred and nineteen," came the reply.

"Whom did you marry?"

"James Webb."

"What was his trade?"

"He traded woollen drapery," she answered.

"When did you first occupy this building?"

"In the year sixteen hundred and forty six."

"What were the names of your children?" I asked.

"Henrietta—James—Ellen, and Anne and Charles," she answered.

"When did you die?" After a long pause, she replied:

"I passed away in the year of Our Lord sixteen hundred and seventy three." And then, "I beg of you to pray for my spirit."

"From what did you die?" I asked.

"A poor fever."

When I asked her what kind of fever seized her there came no answer.

"Where," I asked her, "did your husband James trade?"

"He traded from Butchers Row and Hog Lane."

"What do you think of this house since you left it?" The question she seemed to find difficult to understand, and she answered that she did not like the noise. After this she left with no more to say and I lost contact with her.

Sometime later a voice said:

"Here am I. Here is Thomas."

"Thomas who?" I wanted to know.

"Yea, Thomas Salmon."

"When were you born?"

"I was born of Thomas and Mary in the year fifteen hundred and sixty-eight."

"To whom were you married?"

"My dear Rachel."

Shortly after this he too disappeared. Almost immediately after he had gone, a Richard Webb began to speak. He told me that he had married a Mistress Anne Thyson, that he was a gentleman farmer, and that he did not know when he was born. After informing me that he had first come into possession of the house in 1688 he broke off his contact.

I appeared to come back to the present and was amazed to find that having started this experiment at 10.45, the time was now past 2.00 a.m. However, eager to know more and despite the fact that I felt tired, I returned to my state of trance.

Not long afterwards I heard:

"Anne. Anne. Here is Anne Willis."

"When were you born?" I asked.

"Seventeen hundred and two," she answered. I asked her whom she married.

"Robert was my husband. Robert Webbe."

"What was Robert's trade?"

"A trader in grain was Robert."

"When did you first occupy the house? Did Robert have the front of the house built?" I asked her.

"Yes. Robert had this builded in October in seventeen hundred and thirty. His fine house." After this she left.

Up until this time I had been left in total darkness and could see nothing. I was only hearing the voices.

Then after Anne Willis had left, the blackness was replaced by a growing lightness, as if dawn was breaking. I found myself standing in our hall, but everywhere it was as though it was broad daylight. I noticed how flat and clean the stone floor was. It was not worn away as I knew it to be in 1971. When I noticed a heavy door opening onto a cobbled courtyard from this hallway I realised that I must be viewing the house as it was when it had just been built in 1731. Furthermore, standing in the open doorway was a young child being supported in a circular cane framework on wheels which was holding the child, in a full-length dress, and helping her to learn to walk by preventing her from falling over. She wheeled around but did not see me. In the courtyard I could discern through the doorway a pile of new-looking red bricks in front of a yellowy-brown wall of a cottage, that I knew to be white.

There was no noise, and on the stairs was a man who appeared to be a carpenter, kneeling in a corner on the second flight of stairs hammering silently. His hair I noticed was gingery and he wore a long leather apron. Like the child, who was no longer visible, he took no heed of me.

The plastered wall above the panelling on the staircase was a striking blue.

Moving from the hallway into the dining room, I was immediately struck by the difference between this room and the one with which I was familiar. The fireplace that I knew to be bare bricks was now plastered and it was noticeably lower. A dog sprawled across the hearth on the floor and did not seem to be aware of my presence. The windows which now have wooden frames, were all leaded; one window now in the dining room appeared to be missing. A large refrectory table was circled with small chairs, which looked particularly rustic, uncomfortable and bare.

Suddenly, I found myself back on my bed fully awake. I wrote this experience down straight away so that it did not become distorted. It was not possible to check on the facts that I recorded, but most of the names were later traced in old parish registers. These people had lived during the seventeenth and eighteenth centuries.

Sometime later, when we had the hallway and staircase decorated, a piece of plaster dropped off the wall near the ceiling. The wall beneath this area was found to be a bright chalky blue colour, the same as I had seen that night. The area where I had observed the child near the doorway was now blocked in and covered with shelves. Subsequently, this section of the wall was opened up again, and the frame of the door I had noticed was found.

Although I felt very tired after the trance experience, I suffered no ill effects. I returned to school on Sunday evening, and expected the previous pattern of events to continue.

I had carried out this experiment on May 22nd, and no poltergeist activity was witnessed until the Thursday of the following week, which was May 27th. For four days all was quiet.

From this date the poltergeist activities seemed to decline. Although the phenomena still continued, they were not as regular nor as violent. George Owen felt that any of the following were possible and he wrote:

"In the majority of poltergeist people the mental phenomena (telepathy, travelling clairvoyance, etc.), do not appear, nor any capacity to control these voluntarily. Some people develop the power of psycho-kinesis without the mental phenomena. In very rare cases the chaotic physical phenomena give place to the mental phenomena as if it were a natural evolution. With Matthew the following different possibilities can happen:

"(1) The powers, whether voluntary or involuntary, may disappear suddenly.

"(2) He may retain them and achieve a high degree of control.

"(3) Most of the phenomena may vanish, but he may be left with one or two capacities,"

I wondered which of these three possibilities might apply to me.

A week later I was writing an essay in my study. I do not remember anybody else being present, and it was a few days before "O" level examinations were due to begin. I do not remember either what the subject of the essay was.

However, I was not finding it easy to write, and I had to keep stopping to think what next I was going to write. As I sat with my pen poised above the paper ready to start writing whatever I thought of next, my hand went down onto the paper in a completely involuntary way and began to write. While thinking about what I was going to write, my mind had wandered from the subject, onto nothing in particular.

I watched, startled, as I wrote words in a handwriting different to my own. Then, becoming momentarily frightened, I pulled my hand away and looked at what I had written. The words were incomprehensible and sprawled across half of the page. I tore up the page almost immediately, and it was not until later that I realised that I must have written "automatically", and that my hand had been used and controlled by an outside influence.

I wondered if this was repeatable, and if it was, how I could do it.

The only way I could think of trying again was to sit down with the intent of allowing my hand to be used for automatic writing. It was also necessary to have witnesses, I thought.

On 6th June I asked six of my schoolfriends to join me in the evening for an experiment.

For ten minutes in a darkened study I sat with a pen in my hand at a desk, hoping to be able to start writing on the paper. To my disappointment nothing happened. Five minutes later I tried again, this time with my pen on the paper, rather than above it.

This seemed to be the secret: soon my hand began to move across the paper, producing a spidery writing in the form of a short sentence that read:

"I need help now. You cannot get me. Help. Please."

Pleased with the result, I tried again and produced in the same handwriting:

"Danger. Stop."

This warning did not dampen my inquisitiveness and I continued. A third sentence appeared which read:

"If you do not you will," and it tailed off into illegible writing, until the next sentence that read:

"5 am not knife."

None of this made any sense, so I wrote on the paper:

"Who is this?"

"Joseph West 1783. Get the dog. I need you to help soon. Fire. Fire. Fire 11th June. I too high so die when I need your help soon. Danger of fire when coot dog. Get me soon I beg you."

The writing became more illegible and I asked the entity to explain further what it meant, and the answer came through:

"See your bed too late when into the fire. Do not get the dog on the 19th June. Glass to be dropped into fire. Get fields on 19th June past second you and get it with you two."

Although I was receiving something, there seemed to be large parts missing. However, I had succeeded in producing some writing that appeared to originate from outside my own consciousness. It surprised and puzzled my friends who were present. After this another discovery was made by three of those who had been present; when they went to their beds shortly afterwards, they found that they were soaking wet inside. Perhaps it was merely coincidence that reference was made in one of the sentences to seeing their beds before it was too late.

After this experiment with automatic writing no poltergeist activity occurred for over thirty-six hours.

Two days later, on carrying out a similar experiment, I received a message in slightly different handwriting from the previous one, and very different to my own:

"Sarah Whiffin was . . . Go to the hedge past the strips at the sixteenth hour and I will appear. I mean the allotments. 1697 was my time. Do not disturb me . . ."

In content this message seemed very similar to the first one; both were seemingly irrelevant and difficult to understand. I was not put off by this, as I was having success in writing something, which I thought if practised and developed, could be quite interesting.

I continued writing such "messages" and they were all similar in content for some time. It was becoming obvious though that whenever I did automatic writing, the poltergeist phenomena would temporarily cease. Within a week or two the messages appeared to become more coherent and I received messages such as:

"Henry Taylor has a fine brown horse in yonder field which I must take to Barnstable fair at first light. She will fall old mare, she will fall by ye bridge if you look out of your windows tonight. Poor beast how she suffered in that storm."

One day I wrote down:

"Je suis Marie Anne Lebourgoir. Je te verrai ce soir dans la pièce Marie Anne Lebourgoir."

The messages mostly seemed to originate from people who had met an unpleasant end or from spirits who could not comprehend that they were no longer living on earth. Two such messages which I received early on illustrate this quite clearly:

"Roger Legault hangs by his wrenched neck in the bottom of my basement. If you find him do not tell the peelers . . ."

Another one in French read:

"J'ai dis que je ne suis pas mort. En Suisse entrain. Non je ne suis pas mort."

We had a half-term break around this time and I took my new discovery home with me, and one evening I passed some time doing automatic writing with my family. Of course with a newly-found talent such as this I was far too ambitious. I was asked to try and communicate with famous people such as Churchill, Elizabeth I Cromwell, etc. When I was asked to try Samuel Pepys, I did receive a message, written in a handwriting that was neither mine, nor think, his. Where this message originated from I do not know. I read:

"I perceive ye weather is most mighty hotte. Indeed so hotte ye very powder runs from my face. This very mighte I goe and have talks with King Charles on the deplorable state of the Navy and the Dutche fleete which we perceive to be to near to ye coaste . . ."

I cannot believe that Pepys would write something so naïve, and the style of the language is not correct.

However, a message that I produced the following day appeared more significant. It was the day of the Ascot races and here was an opportunity to see if I could find out the winners. My great-grandfather, who had died in 1960, eleven years previously, was a racehorse owner and associated with such men as Lord Rosebery, I asked him to give me the names of the winning horses. When the morning paper arrived that day it was put away so that nobody in the family knew the names of the horses concerned. We reasoned that if I were successful and picked out the names of the runners, and hopefully the winners, it would mean that telepathy could be ruled out. When I attempted this experiment I wrote the following down:

"I am not sure but try in this order, Spartan, Shady Fellow, Miss London, Dawn Review, Winter Fair, Sea Rover." It was signed with a "C" (standing for Hayward Collins, my great-grandfather's name). I had indeed succeeded in writing down the names of horses which were competing at the races that afternoon. When we looked later in the newspaper their names were all there.

No one in the house knew the names, which ruled out my subconscious and telepathy.

We waited tensely until the afternoon when the results were announced as follows:

Spartan, placed third.
Shady Fellow, placed first.
Miss London, not placed.
Dawn Review, placed third.
Winter Fair, placed second.
Sea Rover, placed first.

The names of the horses I had been given all finished within the first three, with one exception.

As I did more automatic writing, the quality improved, messages became more coherent, intelligible and literate, although still they were largely concerned with petty matters and often seemed to be trivial. For example:

"Please tell Harriett I am safe. It did not really hurt me. I am safe. One day I will see you many worlds away. Susan Horseman", or: "John has got my spoons. Take them from him before he loses them. They are dear to me and they must not be lost. David Fraser, 1971."

Automatic writing appeared to be the most successful method of controlling or preventing the poltergeist phenomena, and if it looked as though disturbances were imminent, I would sit down and write. Later, it became clear to me the writing was the controlling factor. It appeared that the energy I used for writing had previously been used for causing poltergeist disturbances.

The banishing ritual had obviously failed, but I was prepared to try and do anything to get rid of the poltergeist phenomena. I had come across the automatic writing by accident. Only after some time of experimenting did I realise how effective it was in preventing such disturbing phenomena as we all had experienced in the past.

Soon after I had begun automatic writing, other abilities became apparent:

"It was discovered that Matthew could mind-read, and that each and every person had an aura, made up of various colours, which are indicative of the character of the person. It could be disconcerting to be aware in the presence of Matthew that he can pick up the thread of your thought. Fortunately it takes much energy and concentration on his part so that he does not keep up this activity perpetually." (Matron's Report.)

Approaching me one evening on the school campus was another boy whom I did not know; I was walking by myself and I think that I had drifted off almost to the state in which I was accustomed to carry out automatic writing. I was shocked out of this state by seeing to my surprise that the boy was encircled in a pear-shaped aura of colours that looked very much like coloured heat waves. As soon as I came out of my "stupor" the colours vanished, and the boy walked past.

I discovered that I could switch myself "on" or "off" like an electric light-switch. If I switched myself "on" as though I was going to write, but without actually doing so, I could see auras surrounding people. I cannot describe in words how I achieve this switching on and off.

Certain colours in an aura appeared to denote a particular trait in a person's character. By finding out what colours surrounded people that I knew well, I found that each colour was representative of a particular facet of their character. I distinguished six basic colours: blue, green, orange, purple, red and yellow. If someone had a predominantly fiery or temperamental character, then the predominant colour in their aura was red. If they were also kind and generous, they might have this red bordered by blue or purple. Very few people had all six colours. In most cases the bands of colour were limited to two or three, and in some rare cases four.

For some reason, unknown to myself, the clarity and intensity of these colours varies a great deal from one person to another. An interesting observation I have made is that the aura is particularly evident and clear when it surrounds anyone who has any degree of psychic gifts, especially if they are in the habit of using it. Around those who are ill or have a major ailment, it is often weak, and I have noticed that a darker coloured shadow surrounds any area of the person's body that is diseased or affected by illness. If, for example, someone has a tumour, it will darken the aura around the area in which it is sited.

Occasionally if a group of friends were assembled in a relaxed manner in a room, and I was present, I would persistently say whatever someone else was about to say, in the same words that they were about to use. This I discovered in a purely accidental way, and it became obvious that if I switched on and concentrated on a person I could pick up their train of thought, which many of my friends found most disconcerting, especially when I told them of matters concerning themselves that only they knew about. Again, it was much easier to do this with some people than it was with others.

The obvious way to test the accuracy of this mind-reading was to employ a pack of zener cards, which was duly done. The instructions on a packet of zener cards read:

"A. Psychological Conditions.

"1. A pleasant, informed test atmosphere is essential. The subject, or person tested, should be interested and confident. Appeal to his competitive spirit—get him to beat chance.

"2. Encouragement for any success is helpful.

"3. Avoid long sessions; it is extremely difficult to maintain enthusiasm and interest over long periods.

"4. Always allow subject to work at his preferred speed.

"B. Experimental Conditions.

"1. Shuffle the cards carefully, and cut them before each run. A run is 25 trials, once through the pack. A new pack should be thoroughly shuffled.

"2. All shuffling should be screened from the subject, as should cutting and handling. A piece of cardboard, placed on the table between experimenter and subject will serve to conceal the cards during the test.

"3. The subject should be told of his success or failure only at the end of the run and must be allowed only on trial per card.

"4. In serious testing, a minimum of 4 runs per subject is essential . . .

"5. During the check-up *the experimenter* himself should watch and double check the recording."

Zener cards are a deck of cards: twenty-five cards—five each of different designs. The designs are very simple and easy to memorise: a circle, a square, a set of wavy lines, a star and a cross. The point of E.S.P. testing is to find whether or not one person can "guess" what is in another person's mind a greater number of times than would be expected by chance. Going through the pack of zener cards the average right guesses would be five per twenty-five cards.

Among ourselves we tested each other with these cards, according to the instructions. The results of my friends were, with the occasional exception, average. The results that I achieved when tested swung from one extreme to the other. On one set of four runs, I may guess correctly only about six out of one hundred cards, which was far below the average. Yet sometimes I guessed correctly twenty-two, or even twenty-four cards out of twenty-five. Usually I was found to correctly guess between nine and fifteen cards out of twenty-five. Success in E.S.P. cards testing is estimated as follows:

No. of runs of 25 trials	Chance	Fair success (Odd 20+ to 1)	Excellent results (odd 250+ to 1)
4	20	28	32
10	50	63	69
50	250	279	293
100	500	540	560

One evening as I picked up a cup of coffee I received a startling electric shock from the handle. I was taken so much by surprise that I knocked the cup over and spilled its contents. Perhaps I would have thought no more of it, but for the fact that the following day I had the same experience, on placing my hand on a door handle.

This phenomenon continued at odd and unexpected times for a period of nearly a year. It seemed that almost any object had the ability to give me a small electric shock, whether it was metal or another material. I remember receiving such electric shocks from books, windows and even whilst hodding strawberries. On one occasion I put my hand in a large open refrigerator in a shop to lift out a can of soft drink. To the surprise of the watching shopkeeper I dropped it almost immediately I had picked it up, as it gave me such a shock.

I never found any obvious explanation for the electric shocks that I received from assorted objects.

The remainder of the summer term passed without too much disturbance as the poltergeist phenomena gave way to the automatic writing. Obviously there were still some physical disturbances, but in comparison to what had previously been experienced, they were rather unspectacular.

I carried out an interesting experiment near the beginning of that term. I wondered what the results of my "O" level exams would be, disregarding my personal bias towards certain subjects. On a slip of paper I jotted down the grades of the results of all examinations I was to take. I sealed them in an envelope, and gave them to my parents so that I could not at a later date alter anything I had written. I sat for six "O" levels during term, and on examination, three months later and after receiving the results, it was discovered that I had given the correct grade in every case.

The computer readings on the E.E.G. while Matthew was carrying out experiments have been described as staggering. The far-reaching consequences of the results obtained are in Prof. Owen's official report.

CHAPTER V

DURING the summer of 1971 I had much time to devote to carrying out experiments with automatic writing. Much of it was devoted to communicating with a gentleman by the name of Robert Webbe. He had built the front of the house in which we now live in 1731, and he had died shortly afterwards in 1733.

"Matthew says Webbe obviously seems to be still attached to the house he designed. Webbe has actually been 'seen' by Matthew on four or five occasions and he says other people in the house have 'smelt his tobacco or heard his footsteps'.

"Webbe seems to be of an autocratic disposition and when he becomes dissatisfied with Matthew's output of transmitted writings appears to resort to poltergeist activity . . ." wrote *The Psychic Researcher* in July, 1973.

It was becoming increasingly obvious that if the spirits these messages purported to originate from, were in fact in another "world", then they were quite capable of seeing and commenting upon anything that happened in this world. This was illustrated on such occasions when I received messages containing references to events of which they could have had no knowledge whilst they were alive. The following example purports to come from my maternal grandfather who died in 1958:

"Glad to see you spent the money on a car. Just as I would have done. Sorry about Anne. Good luck with the house. God bless you. Golf use my clubs they get dusty. Poor Lionel what a mistake. Good friend. Look after the garden. Enjoy life."

Although the writing was more angular than my grandfather's handwriting while he was alive, the signature was identical. The content of the message was relevant to our life at that time. His consuming interests while he was alive were cars and golf; my mother bought a car with money that he had left to her, and in our cellar were his golf-clubs, which no one ever used as no one else in the family played golf. We were in the process of renovating our old house, and his wife had remarried a close friend of his called Lionel.

There was nothing in that particular message that I did not already know, but I have since received many messages concerning events of which I had no knowledge.

The messages I was writing down varied tremendously from the sublime to the ridiculous. Perhaps this could be accounted for by the fact that they purported to come from a whole range of persons; in fact, from Joe Bloggs to Bertrand Russell. It seemed that unless I asked a specific question that required an answer, the contents of the messages were irrelevant, petty and often just nonsense. The lower end of this spectrum seemed to attract departed alcoholics and victims of car accidents who relayed messages to the effect that the bottle killed them, that they were not in pain, or that their death was quick and without suffering. The upper end attracted such people as Bertrand Russell, to whom I posed the question:

"Have your views on life after death changed since you died, or do you still believe that there is no life after death?"

For some reason I had always thought his christian name was spelt "Bertram", and as I always wrote on the top of the paper the name of the person I wished to communicate with, this is what I wrote down, in addition to the question.

I received the following answer:

"Life returns on its way into a mist, its speed is its quietness again: existence of this world of things and men renews ultimately their never needing to exist. Again knowledge will study others, wisdom is self-known and muscle masters brothers; self-mastery is bone; content may never need to borrow, ambition will wander blind, and as vitality cleaves to the marrow leaving death behind. The universe is deathless because having no infinite self it stays infinite. Clarity has been manifest in heaven and purity in the spirit. Man has no death to die. Bertrand Russell."

The name was signed correctly, whereas if I had written the message I would have written it incorrectly. The reader must judge whether or not this is a message from whom it purports to originate. If it is, then his ideas have been altered by his post-mortal experiences; it is strange that he should use the structure of the human body as an allegory whilst writing on a spiritual subject.

Another curious communication I received was a recipe that was allegedly transmitted by Mrs. Beeton. It read quite simply:

"Ingredients
          Brace of partridge
          Oil or butter
          Two slices of lean ham
          Clove or garlic
          One tomato
          Six mushrooms
          Four clothes
          Six peppercorns
          Salt
          Water or stock.

"Cut your bigger birds into joints or halves, leave pigeons whole. Brown in fat. Put into stew pan and add ham, garlic, tomato, mushrooms, pepper corns, salt and enough water or stock to cover them. A glass of port or red wine may be added. For two hours slowly simmer birds till tender. Serve on dish etc."

Fanny Cradock commented on this recipe in *The Psychic Researcher*:

"The recipe was handed to me and I was asked to comment. Clearly it was not written by a professional chef. The quantities are vague or totally absent. The alternative ingredients include such items as water, scarcely ever used by chefs except for basic stock, the dissolving of gelatine and similar 'basics'. Had this been a chef's recipe the alternatives of stock or water (as with oil or butter) would have been unthinkable. For the former the fluid would be *jùs-de-viande* or *consommé;* while for the latter, oil or butter would have been specified. No quantities are given for either anyway! The incidence of peppercorns is far too high, the size of garlic clove and whether peeled and crushed or used to 'piquer' is not stated. Without labouring the point this a fourth rate recipe, given by someone totally inexperienced in practical cookery.

"Having made these comments I was told the recipe purported to be from Mrs. Isabella Beeton. *This I regard as one of the most evidential examples of automatic writing I have ever seen*! Mrs. Beeton was a hard working journalist. Her husband, Sam Beeton, was the first of the great publicists. He made her and she and he compiled her original 'Mrs. Beeton's Book of Household Management' from recipes sent to them by readers of their threepenny magazine, who were invited to enter a competition. Thus for a one guinea First Prize, a ten shilling Second Prize and a five shilling Third Prize the Beetons were able to compile the recipes which appear in the aforementioned book. Research disclosed that Mrs.

Beeton died aged 29, managed to attend practically every race meeting in England throughout her adult years when not confined with one of her children or suffering from ill health. Yet had she cooked for $31\frac{1}{2}$ hours daily, every day of her life from the time she was $2\frac{1}{2}$, she could only have cooked *once* every recipe published in the original MSS and honest recipe testing prior to publication does not yield 100% satisfaction from first testing.

"In fact there is only one extant record of Mrs. Beeton ever having cooked anything. This came from her sister aged eight who stated, 'she made a cake which turned out more of a biscuit and was a sad failure'."

Mrs. Cradock's comment speaks for itself.

By this time I was receiving nearly as many messages in foreign languages, as in English. The only difficulty here was that I was unable to translate them, as the only other language that I had any degree of knowledge of was French. This meant that I could not tell the content of the messages. The languages included Italian, German, Greek, Latin, Russian, Arabic and various Eastern tongues, as well as old English or Saxon. Many of the messages appeared at first sight to be fragments of existing works, or reproductions of someone else's work, although this is difficult to ascertain. I received, for example, a message that was signed "William Falconer 1801" that read:

> "As some fell conqueror, frantic with success,
> Sheds over the nation's ruin and distress;
> So while the wat'ry wilderness he roamed,
> Incens'd to sevenfold rage the foams;
> And o'er the trembling pines, above, below,
> Shrills through the cordage howls, with woe."

Perhaps this was written not by William Falconer, but by somebody else. Like so many of the scripts, it was irrelevant and apparently pointless. One of the messages I received in French read in prose form:

"Je dis: aux grandes maux les grandes remèdes ou après la mort le medecin qui dit que la patience est un remède à tous maux. Marchand qui perd ne peut rire parce que les plus courtes folies sont les meillures. Jacques Chaumont. 1933." Translated it reads:

"I say: a desperate disease must have a desperate cure or after death comes the physician who says that patience is a plaster for all sores. Let him laugh that wins because the shortest follies are the best."

It reads like a string of proverbs written in French.

Matthew had his first experience of automatic writing at the age of fifteen.
During the writing of an essay, he suddenly noticed an involuntary movement
of his hand; he was writing without knowing what was appearing on the paper
in front of him. Simultaneously, the poltergeist phenomenon decreased. Soon
Matthew realised that he could control the poltergeist manifestations by
allowing himself to be used as a channel for automatic writing. Since then
Matthew has taken down many hundreds of automatic messages. The most
striking feature of Matthew's automatic writing is the variety of handwritings,
scripts and languages in which he takes down the messages. Robert Webbe is
a prolific communicator and so is a Thomas Penn who gives medical diagnoses.
From time to time Matthew has tried to establish contact with a specific
person; the result is then sometimes banal and by no means evidential, but
still quite interesting, as in this brief communication from someone signing
herself "Anne R. 1708 Jan".

*This desease I feel to be most
agonising and if physicians do
nothing for my curled pos.
Anne R.
1708 Jan.*

75

I died in Switzerland on April 21 1952. I am now restless. My body is at Sapperton Where is Frith Hill? In the storm and uncertainty and fear that today permeate the world, set yourselves to become part of the — hand of God which stretches out — to bring peace and patience and high standards of truth and justice to all peoples. Bless my body and allow mass. Here is Charles, father now. I must go

Richard Cripps

52
T.

This communication was written down by Matthew without premeditation It was not until Matthew's father saw this letter that it was realised wh— purported to be the writer:

"I died in Switzerland on April 21 1952. I am now restless. My body is a— Sapperton. Where is Frith Hill? In the storm and uncertainty and fear tha— today permeate the world set yourselves to become part of the hand of Go— which stretches out to bring peace and patience and high standards of trut— and justice to all peoples. Bless my body and allow mass. Here is Charle— father now. I must go.
                                    Richard Cripps
                                         5²
                                          T"

Bertram Russell.

Have your views on life after death changed since you died? Or do you still believe that there is no life after death?

Life returns on its way into a mist, its speed is its quietness again: existence of this world of things and men renews ultimately their never needing to exist. Again knowledge will study others — wisdom is self-known and muscle masters brothers, self-mastery is bone; content may never need to borrow; ambition will wander blind and as vitality cleaves to the marrow leaving death behind. The universe is deathless because having no infinite self it stays infinite. Clarity has been manifest in heaven and purity in the spirit. Man has no death to die.

Bertrand Russell

Knowing of Lord Bertrand Russell's material outlook when alive, Matthew addressed himself to the late philosopher. However, he believed his name to be BERTRAM. The message is signed BERTRAND Russell.

"Life returns on its way into a mist, its speed is its quietness again: existence of this world of things and men renews ultimately their never needing to exist. Again knowledge will study others—wisdom is self-known and muscle masters brothers, self-mastery is bone; content may never need to borrow; ambition will wander blind and as vitality cleaves to the marrow leaving death behind. The universe is deathless because having no infinite self, it stays infinite. Clarity has been manifest in heaven and purity in the spirit. Man has no death to die.

Bertrand Russell"

77

During a photographic session at the offices of "The Psychic Researcher"
Matthew took down a message which he threw into a wastepaper basket after
the photographs had been taken. Later the message was taken out because he
had mentioned in conversation that his hand had been moved with great
force while the pictures were taken. The message was addressed to a person
called Tom; the writer purported to be Tom's brother who had been killed
by a mine off the shores of Norway, and he signed himself Johanson.—Hours
later, a member of the "Researcher's" staff suggested that Tom Johanson,
the General Secretary of the Spiritualist Association, was probably the intended
recipient. Mr. Johanson said on the telephone in answer to the question
whether he had a brother: "No—" and after a moment, "mind you I had
one, but he was reported missing during the war. He was a sailor in the
Norwegian Navy."

78

"One morning Matthew came to me and said he had a visitation during the night, and this happened three times thereafter. He then described the woman he had seen, and after this I told him he had nothing to worry about, as it could, according to all he said of her, be my mother, who passed away on August 12th.

"He produced a piece of paper, on which was a message from my mother, Jeanne Cracknell. She had spoken to Matthew one evening, telling him not to worry and that she was only interested. She had known before her death of Matthew's dilemma and his gifts. She also was aware that I had E.S.P. and took it all as perfectly natural.

"I received through Matthew three messages unmistakably in her style. She wanted her possessions kept in good hands, which I had already seen to, and she wanted to say that I was not to worry about her as she was safe. Matthew had seen her as she was when she died and she looked exactly the same as when I had seen her pass away..." (Matron's report.)

One night during the first week of my return to school, I awoke for no apparent reason at about one o'clock, feeling the same cold that I had sensed on previous occasions. I was sleeping in a small dormitory of some seven younger boys, being myself in charge of them. It was the same room in which the illuminated crucifix and crown of thorns had been witnessed.

The door was open, and yet I remembered having closed it properly. In the darkness I could see the vague form of a person about twelve feet from my bed. As it came nearer to my corner of the room, I could make out that it was in a stooping, rounded position, and was nobody that I recognised. I was still "bathed" in this coldness, even though I was in bed, and to my dismay this figure was slowly approaching my end of the room.

When the figure arrived at the foot of my bed I could see that it was a woman; she was elderly and hunched up. Her hair was tied up in a bun at the back of her head. After a few moments she faintly smiled, lifted a hand, and vanished.

I happened to mention this to the Matron on the following day, and she was quite unconcerned, saying it was her mother. She described to me her mother and later found a photograph of her. The lady had died some five weeks ago and I recognised her as the same person whom I had seen in the night.

She had been ill before her death, and this had caused her to adopt the stooping position I had seen. During her illness, while she was being nursed, she had always requested that her bedroom door be left open at night, so that if necessary she could call out for help.

During the two subsequent nights, I again saw her under the same circumstances, when she would shuffle across the dormitory to the end of my bed, where she would stand, as if to look at me, then raise her hand and disappear. After she appeared three times I did not see her again. I was, it seemed, the only person that saw her on these occasions, perhaps because I was the only occupant of the room who was awake.

Occasionally objects that once belonged to her and were now being looked after by the Matron, would move, so that they were in a prominent position in the middle of the room. We could see no obvious reason for this, other than the fact that she wanted to make her presence known.

A few days later a large pool of light appeared sporadically for some weeks at night on the ceiling above my bed. I decided to try and find out the reason for this occurrence by automatic writing. Fairly soon, in a garbled message, I was told that Anne Chapman was wanting help, that she had been trying to attract someone's attention. Annie, as she called herself, told her story through my pen.

The house was built in the late 1880's and she had been employed as a servant in this household that was familiar with balls and entertainment; the house was apparently a country lodge at this time and was owned by a wealthy farmer. For some reason that she would not disclose, she had attempted to take her life in 1890, by hanging herself but had failed, although she had succeeded in choking herself nearly unconscious. She had been found by a man known as William, or Bill, who was in some way connected with her attempted suicide. He cut the rope and had taken her down. Then he dragged her from one end of the house to the other taking her down a flight of back stairs to the scullery, where he finally took her life by depositing her limp body, head first, in a barrel of water, where she drowned.

The horror of this atrocity caused her spirit to be restless, and she was still haunting the rooms and corridors of the house. She asked me in writing to help her by placing for one night a vessel of water on top of a Bible in a particular room, so that she could find peace.

I did this and the light on the ceiling never appeared again. Her murderer, a man named William, manifested himself on several occasions.

Although I had no wish or intention to associate with such entities, it now began to look as if my very presence acted like a magnet for those who wanted to communicate. Being near a place where some evil deed had been committed in the past, seemed to provoke the principle parties to re-enact the happening through my pen. Often I was practically forced to write, though I tried to resist the urge as strongly as I could.

CHAPTER VI

DURING the winter of 1970 and early spring I had been compiling a work on the Webbe family of our village for an "O" level history project from contemporary sources held in the Cambridgeshire Public Records Office.

My father owns a set of four tradesmen's tokens from our village. There is a halfpenny bearing the name Robert Halls, and dated 1667, a token of John Bittin, dated 1657, a token of John Harvey, and a token of Robert Moore dated 1667. I also wanted to find some information concerning these names. Searching through the records I soon discovered that there were fewer famiiles than I expected but they were larger; many generations and family branches lived in one village, and often under one roof. The names that were predominant in the documents I was searching amongst were Tofts, Hockley, Onyon, Moore, Bittin, Whiffin, Paris, Milicent and Webbe.

The name Webbe was of particular interest to me, more so than the four names of the tradesmen, because, scratched into a brick on an outside wall of our house is the name "John Webbe 1731". On other bricks can be found similar engraved initials such as "J.K.K.", "J.P. 1799", "J.E.", and "T.W.". We knew that a family named Webbe had occupied the house at some time, and I therefore looked for further information concerning the Webbes. Documents and references concerning this name were not scarce, and I quickly built up a mass of information. But there were also large sections and periods that were missing and not on record. These missing pieces meant that in many of the facts I had gathered were unconnected and therefore incomplete. I could not, for example, produce a complete family-tree because many names were not recorded on the documents.

However, I ascertained conclusively that the Webbe family originated from a neighbouring village in the early sixteenth century and had come fortune-hunting in our village, which at that time was a wool town, growing in prosperity in the same way as many other surrounding towns and villages.

The Webbe family flourished and grew very rapidly, gaining wealth and land. This prosperity reached a peak when a certain Richard Webbe, Gentleman, owned eleven shops and a considerable amount of land. He died in 1708. It is often said that a family fortune is lost in three generations and that applied to this family; Robert Webbe, the eldest son of Richard, inherited the fortune and sold some of the property. When his son, also named Robert, died in 1756 his trade was described in records as a glazier. From that time on the family's fortunes declined.

My presence in our house, once occupied for nearly three hundred years by successive generations of Webbes, seemed to bring about the appearance of a certain Robert Webbe. As soon as I began to write out the notes I had made on his family.

Some of the first automatic writings I received purported to come from someone that signed himself "Rob: Webbe 1733". Over a period of about one year he wrote through my hand nearly fifty pages of foolscap, talking about his everyday life during the early years of the eighteenth century. In addition, in these writings he claimed responsibility for many inexplicable happenings, including the arrival of a variety of apported objects that were found around the house. After he had written several thousand words through my hand, he appeared to develop a power to write of his own volition, and without my hand being used to hold and guide the pen.

My mother is in the habit of writing on a scrap of paper the meals that she plans to prepare during the forthcoming week. On one occasion she jotted down on an envelope the days of the week, when she was called away, before completing the menu. The pencil was left on top of the paper. When she returned sometime later the envelope had written on it, in Webbe's characteristic handwriting:

"Wednesday. I would say ye smalle woode doves stuffed with almonde.

"Friday. For this day I fancey carpe and sauce of pea.

"Saturday. A side of tender pig from my man Rob: Moore for 2/2 and spiced stuffing.

"Sunday. For this day have a goodley meal. Perchance ye swanne and pike fillets with ducke purchased from good Rob Moore. From my good man Robert Moore some 9d. for a whole fish."

When my mother showed me the envelope I took a pen and wrote down myself that a pound of bacon cost 7 shillings and 8 pence (reverting from decimal currency which Robert Webbe would not comprehend). To this he replied immediately, using my hand holding the pencil:

"This is moste mightey disreputable. I buy a whole hogg from Rob: Moore for 7 shillings."

Telling him that one dozen large hens' eggs cost 6 shillings, he replied:

"I cannot believe this. I had my own foul(!) but eggs cost 2d. only for twelve. Mr. Moore."

His reaction when I told him that a coat and breeches, hand-made by a tailor, cost around £50, was:

"This is moste distressing. I purchase a fine coat, breeches, stockinges, and fine hat for £6, in Cambridge."

The following transcript of a "conversation" I held with him is typical. It shows his complete inability to understand life as I know it, or of being able to grasp any matter outside his own past environment. Everything I wrote had to be explained in terms that he could perhaps follow. He had no knowledge of cars, so I described them as "horseless carriages"!

"It takes us twenty minutes to travel to Cambridge in our horseless carriage."

"It takes me some one hour or more across a bad road and much wilde land covered in part by wood."

"You can fly to France in twenty minutes."

"This cannot be true. Birds are the only creatures to fly and it takes some three days to cross to France. I cannot believe such ridicule and nonsense."

"I have flown to the Mediterranean in three and a half hours."

"Indeed I see you are a fine jester. Do not tell me such stories. Perhaps Barnardes son can ride a cammell."

"I am not jesting. I only tell the truth."

"I begin to doubt you. Indeed I have a tame lion who guards my house while he stands on ye roofe."

When I explained to him that a car was a horseless carriage he replied:

"I have never heard of the like of such nonsense for a long time. All carriages must have a horse else they stand still."

His presence became somewhat unwelcome on occasions, especially when he began to light candles we have in our house, regardless of their position or fire risk. One evening a candle in a holder was found burning steadily on the floor of a cloakroom. I asked him why he lit our candle.

"This I must admit to having being done. I should expres my gratitude for you giving to me in my roome these fine candles which are so much better than those that I have. These candles make so little much smoke."

I then asked him why he placed a candle in such an unlikely position as on the floor in the water closet.

"I know not the water closette you tell me of," he wrote, "but I did place my candles in my servery which was lacking in ye same."

How, I asked, did he light the candles?

"Why that is either by means of tinder-boxe or by ye fire in ye rooms. This is done how I always lite my candles."

Certain household objects were noticed to have disappeared. This we thought could be poltergeist phenomena, although it seemed somehow unlikely as these items were not found again. Also we frequently found another object which no one had seen before, just after one of our belongings had vanished. We had thus presented to us over some months many objects, including a late eighteenth century book, which we found page by page over a period of six weeks in the summer of 1971, a small old loaf that was very heavy for its size and literally as hard as concrete; a fossil with Robert Webbe's name scratched on it, an old bees wax candle, a diamond-shaped pane of glass and other items. None of these had been seen before, they just "arrived", never to be witnessed materialising. It seemed likely that Webbe was removing our objects himself, and in turn giving us items that we presumed he had taken, perhaps from previous famiiles occupying the house. The objects were rarely contemporary with Webbe's lifetime, although many of them were obviously old. Our idea of the objects originating from Webbe was supported when he wrote:

"Now that you ask I shall have to profess to having founde certayne articles such for example being a fine neckerchief, and some of which I know not what they are, but I keepe them in myne pockets or give to my friendes."

"What else have you got?" I asked him.

"I have also that I have found a smallen waxen doll and a fine bone knife, a pinne for a hat, a fine book about methinks one Thomas Jones or some such name, a pretty cloth such as the goodley man John Byttine has never seen the like of."

I asked if he could return them to us.

"I cannot give these to you for so many reasons. First I have got not them all, second some tickle my fancy and thirdlee they are in my house and therefore are by rite to me."

Foolishly I one day told him that we had four tradesmen's tokens to which he replied very quickly:

"I must use such tokens as you can not spend them. If I see them I can use them to pay my provisions for my goode man Robert Moore. This is very fine. I now can pay for my candles and by some potions. I must by some tallow soon."

Within a few days to my father's dismay the tokens had all vanished. Fortunately I managed to persuade Webbe to return them.

86

The "Spirit Graffiti" of Queens House are among the most unusual psychic phenomena ever to have manifested themselves. Between 31 July and 6 August 1971, five-hundred and three signatures, nearly all with a date, appeared on the walls of Matthew's bedroom. Doors and windows were securely locked while inside the room strange scratching noises indicated that "somebody" was writing on the wall. Many of the names have later been traced in the parish records of Linton. The original owner of the house, a Robert Webbe, who died in 1733, had indicated through automatic writing to Matthew that he would bring "half-a-thousand signatures of friends and family".

Nobody ever saw the pencils move; several of them were left in the room. Signatures were found in the most inaccessible places, on the ceiling and even on the lampshade. The large letters are markings put there for research purposes. (Below) This sketch shows the location of Matthew's bedroom; the majority of the graffiti are on one wall.

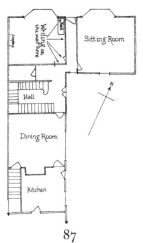

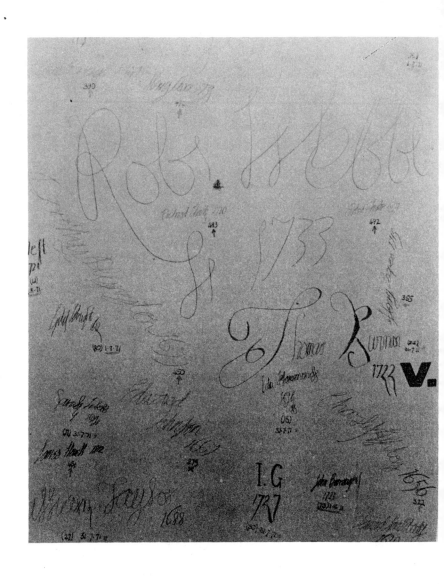

Robert Webbe 1733—signed twice. However, he added six poems to the other writings on the wall which he also signed. All of Robert Webbe's pieces are dated 1733. The other signatures bear dates from 1355 to 1870.

William Nicholas, R.I.B.A.,   Cambridge

Being a friend and professional colleague of the author's father, and having on numerous occasions, expressed an interest in the extraordinary events surrounding his family, it was not without some inner feeling of excitement and expectancy, that I set out to visit Linton early one afternoon. This visit was prompted by an invitation to witness, with my own eyes, the alleged culmination of several hours hard work put in by an unknown agency. This agency was supposedly the erstwhile essence/spirit, energy or "what-you-will" of one Robert Webb, a former owner and resident of Queen's House, Linton, the destination of my visit. Robert Webb had been selflessly employed, in an apparently pointless task, of collecting together a vast amount of signatures—autographs. These signatures had been culled from persons long since deceased and generously applied to the various parts of the panelled wall surfaces of the author's bedroom.

Having hurried over, anxious not to miss anything, it was surprising to find the complete lack of excitement and utter calm which pervaded the house. They all had, of course, been living within the environment of scientifically unexplainable and therefore strange events for many years.

I was taken into Matthew's room and shown the multitude of very interesting signatures which decorated the whole of one and a part of the other adjoining wall.

These writings, executed with precision and care, using a black pencil, stood out clearly on the white painted wall.

Furthermore, Matthew had marked each and every new appearance with coloured ink, thus recording date, time and order of arrival.

Having carefully examined the signatures I was accompanied by the entire household into the sunlit gardens. It being explained that the phenomena did not and would not occur whilst the wall was under direct observation. A pencil was left, however, hopefully on the bed.

Some seven to ten minutes later we returned to find that another new signature had been added.

This was then, and still is, one of the most interesting and mystifying direct experiences of my life. I am grateful that I was given the opportunity of being a witness to this extraordinary event.

We were again dismayed a few days later when on my bedroom wall one Saturday morning appeared in large writing "Rob: Webbe".

Shortly after we had found this name, another one in more controlled writing appeared, saying the same thing. An hour later yet another appeared, this time reading "Hannah Webbe 1652".

"Tell Webbe that he is not to write on our walls. We've got enough to do without him making more work," I was told by my father.

"I will write as I like. They are my walls and this is my house," retorted Webbe.

Within fifteen minutes another name had appeared, "Thomas Webbe 1620."

By midday about fifteen names had been scrawled on the white-painted panelled wall. They were in varying handwritings. Again I communicated with Robert Webbe to ask him why he was writing these names on the wall.

"Indeed I did see your own fine workes on my familye," he claimed, "and did decide to help you by allowing my friendes and family to sign their name on ye wall. You must realise that this is my wall and I am at libertye to write on mine owne walls. Your worke was most fine and in most part very right."

He promised me "half a thousand" names which he hoped would fill in some of the gaps in my project.

"The writings on the wall appeared during the day and always when the room was empty," wrote *The Psychic Researcher* in the September, 1973, issue. "Pencils were left in the room and found to be blunt from use after each occurrence . . . The actual happenings which took place over a period of six days are extremely well documented; in fact we marked the walls clearly with letters of the alphabet so that progress of this 'spirit convention' could be followed more easily. In one case the letter T was actually incorporated in the design of the writers' names.

"As to the names which appeared: many have been traced in old parish records.

"Why should Robert Webbe be so anxious to call five-hundred witnesses? Matthew feels that this was just one of the occasions when the evidence by its sheer volume appeared to over-power the most sceptical of witnesses.

"Of course there is far more to it than just some graffiti on the walls; seen in context with other communications from Robert Webbe, a definite pattern emerges. But what rôle does Matthew play in this unusual psychic phenomenon? 'Matthew appears to be a catalyst,' said one of the psychologists presently involved with an examination of the case."

Robert Webbe kept to his promise and five hundred and three names were written on the walls; included in these names were some Continental signatures, presumably of merchants, with such names as Johann Oubonnet and Hugo Beaumont. Each was accompanied by a date which seems to have no particular relevance, except that in some cases I found it to be the date of death of the person. The great majority of the names are familiar village family names.

Mr. Webbe died, it seems, from a disease of his legs; in every other message from him comes a complaint about his maladies. He still thinks that he is alive and that he owns the house—he is not sure why we live in it. There is a particularly dogmatic streak in his character that is well illustrated by the following passage when I tried to make him believe it was 1972 and not 1727, as he so fervently believed.

"If ye yeare is 1972 then shall I be resting under ye cold stones. It has been ye yeare of our Lord 1727 for close on foure months. Perhaps next you can tell me I am living on ye church tower with ye Deville."

It was interesting that at the time I "wrote" this, it was April 1972, and so I informed him that it had been 1972 for four months. In reply came:

"I cannot explain this to you. Our King George came to the throne in 1714, which makes some 27

　　　　　　　　　　14

　　　　　　　　　　13 yrs. Do you doubt our Royal Majestie's Reign or are you a bumpkin."

After about twelve months he became so impetuous, unintelligible and erratic in his statements that I devoted my energy to more constructive ends.*

During a half-term break in my Autumn Term in 1971, it was suggested by my mother that I tried to communicate with an artist and ask him to draw for me a picture. She ventured that I might try Sir Alfred Munnings, the famous equestrian painter; horses are one of the most difficult animals to draw, and she knew that my own drawing ability would prevent me from drawing one myself.

All I had to draw with was a pencil and a piece of paper. I sat down and adopted the same procedure as though I was about to write automatically. I concentrated on the request that Alfred Munnings draw for me a horse.

* During the writing of this chapter on September 20th, 1973, a message was found on a cupboard door in the kitchen, signed by Webbe and reading:
"I see you write fun of me and mocke me. I see you write of me."

One hour later the piece of paper had been filled with a strange scene, in the centre of which was a horse.

The picture was not particularly good—in fact the only thing that was of any little artistic merit was the horse itself. The rest of the picture was a badly drawn desolate dead scene.

There was a girthed horse tied from a bridle to a dead stump on a flat, hollow looking dead tree. In fact the whole picture was seemingly dead, the only living thing in it appeared to be the animal. It was sinister and for some while it frightened me. Behind the horse was another dead tree. Stiff, dead looking grass stood in rigid fans around on the flat lifeless ground which was strewn with large hard stones. The sky down to the horizon was black, stormy and oppressive. I knew I had not drawn this picture with my own hand. I could never have drawn the horse.

This happened on 2nd November, 1971.

The same day I "drew" a camel apparently under the guidance of the wood-cutter Thomas Bewick, who died in 1826. Artistically, the camel was better than the horse that came from Munnings—it was not so flat. To my disappointment, I had no energy left with which to carry on communicating, and I reluctantly stopped drawing.

Later in the week I produced a pencil drawing of a swan and a small feather, purporting to come from Thomas Bewick. The artistic standard of drawings was improving.

After I had returned to school for the rest of the Autumn Term, I received several more drawings, all in pencil, and purporting to originate from a variety of artists who were dead, some anonymous, some signing their signatures.

When I had been doing these automatic drawings for about a month, the quality of the content of the writings improved as well. The quality of the drawings had improved much faster than the writing.

I received several messages in automatic writing from persons who would often give me an address and the name of a living person they wished me to pass on a message to. Obviously I was not in a position to do so. These messages would take the form of the following, which I have invented myself and is not a genuine message. It is only designed to explain the type of message I received:

"I died in St. Hilary's Hospital, Castle Rise, on Tuesday, 19th November. My wife is grieving for me and is miserable. Please tell her that I am safe and happy. I have met John and Jessie. I send my love to the children Susan, David and Richard. Please contact my wife Doris at 4, Pollard Avenue, Furnby."

It could be said that I was reading obituaries in daily newspapers, and then, consciously or unconsciously, reproducing them in automatically written texts. But at this time at school I read no newspapers except occasionally the *Daily Express* which has no obituary column. It seems to me unlikely therefore that I was merely reproducing something that I had seen before.

On October 8th, 1971, I received a curious message which read:

"He has not long to live. In a week he will be here. Do not hold his head. L.F.M."

Not long after I received this warning, Lionel Frederick Mullis died. He was the second husband of my grandmother. At the time I wrote this message I was unaware of his state of health, and in fact it was not until after his death that this message bore any relevance to the initials L.F.M.

The drawings that I produced caused more and more questions to be asked about their origin and how I managed to draw them, especially as it was well known that I had never possessed any ability to draw or paint. I have already mentioned that many of the drawings were "anonymous", but there were so many different styles expressed in the drawings that this in itself was quite baffling.

By late 1971 I had drawings in the styles of Walt Disney, Bewick, early European woodcutters, and early twentieth century French artists. Similar themes and features could be found in many of the drawings, but they were all translated into the particular style of different artists.

A large proportion of the drawings seemed to feature dead branches and hard stone surfaces, giving them a somewhat sinister appearance.

An owl drawn with my fountain pen, and purporting to be drawn by Thomas Bewick, was attractively executed and then set in a background of protruding dead branches of a tree. The bird itself perched on a stone, displaying large talons and a preying beak.

From an anonymous artist I received a drawing on which was written "VIVE LA FRANCE". This too looked sinister and shows a legless man on a street corner. Behind him on two sides are stone walls; the man is seated on a stone ledge, running off onto a paved road. His hands are deformed and on one side of him is a drain, a bottle, and a lifeless bird. Between the stumps of his legs is a scattering of coins. He has a black beard and his eyes are blacked out to look like dark sockets. He is so positioned on the street corner that all the lines which make up the corners or edges of the walls, the ledges and the road, join at one point in his crutch. On a wall

Thomas Rowlandson

W. Keble Martin

Thomas Bewick

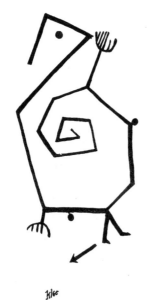

Paul Klee *Henri Matisse (?)*

96

was daubed "Vive La France", the F being written the wrong way round.

By December, 1971, I had been doing automatic writing for nearly five months. Very little poltergeist activity had been witnessed since July; in fact, the only time such a phenomenon occurred was when I had done no writing or drawing for over a week, and then small objects would move about in a mischievous way.

The Matron left the school in early December in order to become manageress of a public house that her father had been managing before her. He was taken ill, and as there was no one else to look after it, she had to leave us. I mention this because several interesting events were connected with both of us later on.

I continued to receive regular automatic messages; their contents varied. Some of them were banal and meaningless, others fascinating and even very intelligent. A Gerald Wood informed me that he thought I would "find the swing of pendulum T given as $T = 2\pi\sqrt{\frac{l}{g}}$" A Martin Warboys hoped that I had "something in the wind".

"Try the old races again, Bert mate," he advised!

I received a particularly sad but interesting communication from a small boy who had been knocked down by a car and killed on a main road a few yards from our house. He had been on his way home from school where he was usually met by his mother; on that particular afternoon there was no one to meet him and he was killed crossing the road unaccompanied.

"Tell Mummy," he wrote in a childish handwriting, "that I am all right but I have not got my front teeth because the car knocked them out." It is important to mention that I did not try to communicate with that boy; his note just appeared with others.

A strange incident happened in January 1972. I went into the town to purchase a gramophone record, "It don't come easy" by Ringo Starr, but was unable to get it in either of the two record shops. Disappointed, I walked back to school, but on entering my study ten minutes later I found a brand new copy in its sleeve on my desk, yet no one in my house at school had one, of that I was certain.

Where had it come from? I still don't know the answer. Did I wish so strongly to have this record that it simply materialised? Was it an apport from one of those who communicated with me?

On later occasions I have experienced similar situations, although I have never been able to force a wish to come true. Usually, I find certain objects if I have wished for them, not consciously in order to obtain them, but subconsciously as part of my thoughts whilst trying to get hold of them in the most natural way.

97

For example, I was collecting material for a Guy Fawkes fire at the bottom of our garden. Finding myself short of rubbish, except for half a dozen cardboard boxes, I went to the house and asked my mother what I could use. There was no one else at home and she had no idea or suggestion. I returned to the bottom of the garden, and to my utter amazement I found a stack of large logs and wood placed next to the cardboard boxes.

At that time there was nobody who could have done this, let alone in the short space of time I had been in the house. In all, there were several hundredweight of wood and logs. The only explanation feasible is that they materialized as a result of my wishing.

The curious thing is that the items that materialize in this fashion are never essentials; they are perhaps useful extras. Other such apports included several gramophone records, a bag of sugar, a bank note, a pair of black lace gloves and postage stamps.

A long-playing record of which I had a copy appeared one day in the house; it seemed to have come from another owner as it bore obvious marks of wear. There seemed no reason for this to materialise as I owned a copy of it already.

Another curious incident occurred on the Brighton to London train. One evening I was returning from Brighton to Cambridge and having eaten nothing all day, I was feeling very hungry. There was no buffet car on the train. I went along to the cloakroom to wash, taking with me a flannel I carried in my bag.

When I returned to my compartment, I put my flannel back into the travelling bag, which I had left zipped and closed. To my surprise there was in the bag a pint bottle of beer and an apple pie; these I gladly consumed.

It is out of the bounds of reality to try and explain this away by suggesting that someone had entered my compartment and put the pie and beer in my bag while I was down the corridor for five minutes. It just would not make sense. As in the case of the firewood, who would have conceivably carried out such a charitable act, and who else could have known that I was hungry? The compartment I occupied was empty except for myself.

One morning I entered my bedroom to find a wad of trading stamps on my bed. I had not, as far as I could recall, been wishing for them, although my mother collects them. When we counted them there were, all on one long band, 680 stamps which according to my calculations would have meant spending £17, or £8.50 in a shop giving double stamps. From where these stamps materialized still remains, as do the other objects, a mystery.

At times my presence seemed to have a most peculiar effect on cars in which I travelled.

On several of the many journeys I have made with my father between Cambridge and my school the engine cut out for no apparent reason, as if the ignition had been switched off. It seemed to be an electrical fault that stopped the engine; we could be travelling along, sometimes at a speed of 70 m.p.h. along the A1, when we suddenly would lose all speed and acceleration. The car came to a halt and refused to start again. The remedy we found after some experience of this was for me to get out of the car, after which the engine would start immediately. This has occurred in three different cars and never happened when I was not a passenger.

One afternoon I lay in a bath at school. Facing me was a window which was firmly closed. On a ledge at the plug end of my bath was an assortment of soap and plugs. From my position, there were in front of me firstly the taps, then the ledge, and a few feet behind the ledge was the window. As I day-dreamed in that direction a plug rose up into the air.

This startled me. It was the first poltergeist phenomenon I had witnessed for some weeks and the first time for many months that I had actually seen an object move.

The plug then shot towards the window with as much speed as though someone had hit it very forcefully with a bat. In fact I thought in a flash that it would shatter the window. To my amazement, it passed through the window and disappeared from sight.

The window remained firmly closed and unbroken.

A few minutes later I found a plug, which I presumed to be the same one, lying on the ground on the other side of the window.

This to me could be an explanation how objects, during the violent poltergeist outbreak of the previous year, had moved from one end of the house to the other, without being seen, often they seemed to have to pass through rooms full of people or shut doors. It could also account for the reason why many household items just vanished at that time, even though they were apparently too large to be merely hidden.

Yet another interesting phenomenon manifested itself onto a tape recorder, on two separate occasions. The first instance occurred at school and was witnessed by five people, and the second incident took place at home during holiday time.

One night I decided with four friends to carry out an experiment along the lines of the Electronic Voice Phenomenon and we all assembled in my study around a large tape recorder at about 11 p.m.

The machine was switched on to record, and the recorder, although plugged in, was turned off after each of us announced our name and asked for a particular person to speak on the tape. When we played back the tape there was nothing but three minutes of silence. Next we asked someone else to talk; again there was no response after three minutes.

An hour later, having still had no success, we decided to have one more attempt and to then go to bed. It seemed that we were not going to get any response.

"Why not try Hitler?" someone suggested. "He is much more likely to work as it is always easier to attract a power of evil than a power of good."

This, at the time, seemed a good idea, so we invited Hitler to speak, and then concentrated on his name while the tape recorder ran for a few minutes.

After we stopped the tape we ran it back to the beginning for play-back.

It began with distant rumbling gunfire, which soon gave way to regimented marching. This continued for nearly a minute, and sounded as though the microphone was placed near to soldiers as they marched past it. Then behind this noise a sound like a brass band could be heard playing a marching tune, which was later identified as one of the German Nazi songs. The marching feet began running as gunfire could be heard more clearly in the background. Still the music kept playing over it all and incoherent shouting was audible.

It then began to sound as though the feet were running down a stone or concrete corridor which produced an echo.

At this point the tape ended.

Startled and amazed we played the tape over and over again. We all had checked the tape carefully beforehand and can swear that it was clean on all four tracks. The microphone was not switched on rendering it useless to record normal sounds.

Curious to see if the experience could be repeated, we switched on the tape recorder again.

Three minutes later there was nothing on the tape, so we began recording again for another three minutes.

I had on my desk an alabaster stone egg. The egg was five feet away from the tape recorder and about eight feet from the microphone.

For no obvious reason this egg, which was on the desk, about eighteen inches from where I was sitting, began to emit a whistling sound which started off as a low "buzzing" and mounted to a noise comparable to an electronic feed-back. Still the tape recorder was switched on.

I put out my hand to pick up the egg, and as soon as I got within an inch of it, the noise intensified to a level that hurt our ears. When I withdrew my hand the noise level receded to a clearly audible whistling tone. One of my friends stretched out to touch the egg and the noise stopped. He picked the egg up and, he said, that it was quite warm; it should not have been warm as it was solid stone, and had not been handled before.

He handed the egg to another friend and it again began to whine. When I took it, the noise rose to its former level until I put it back on the desk where it just continued emitting a low hum.

Whoever touched the egg caused it to produce a different noise which was sometimes a high-pitched whistling sound and sometimes a low humming. The noise increased most when I touched it.

This phenomena continued for just over fifteen minutes. We had started the tape recorder when this whistling started and recorded everything while it went on. When we played it back the noises and our voices were clearly recorded.

The second incident happened at home when I was amusing myself with a cassette tape recorder late in the evening.

Listening to the ten o'clock news on the radio, the newscaster talked about violence in Northern Ireland, bombing and shooting, and the deaths of some soldiers whose patrols had been ambushed.

After the news I went to my room and switched the tape recorder on with the microphone plugged in. I allowed it to record silence for about two minutes and then played it back.

At first it ran silently. I was suddenly shaken by two clearly audible gun shots. There followed another short silence which was soon shattered by two rounds of machine-gun fire. After a couple of seconds these gave way to single shots and much shouting that was incoherent. The sequence of noises ran for nearly forty-five seconds and the remainder of the tape was again quiet. I played this back several times, and my parents listened to it as horrified as I myself was.

I went outside for a walk on my own, and returned home about twenty minutes later.

Again I went to the cassette recorder and switched it on to record, as I was wondering if I would receive some information or perhaps the same sounds again.

Immediately I played back the tape, organ music was clearly audible. It sounded like a pipe-organ and as though I had recorded it inside a church while it played. With my parents I played this

piece of music of about fifteen seconds duration over and over again.
It was nothing we could recall having previously heard, and it really
sounded like a funeral piece of music.

My reaction to the first recording of gunfire had been one of sad-
ness and I had thought of the relatives of the dead soldiers.

I had only gone out for a walk because I felt so sad and miserable
thinking about the young men, just a year older than myself.

Whether these two sequences were related, I don't know. Nor do
I profess to know the answer to questions which have been put to
me by my parents, namely whether I might have projected these
sounds subconsciously onto the tape.

On 2 April, 1972, I received a communication purporting to
come from and signed by Frederick Myers, the well-known psychical
researcher, and one of the founder members of the S.P.R. It read:

"You should not really indulge in this unless you know what you
are doing. I did a lot of work on automatic writing when I was alive
and I could never work it out. No one alive will ever work out the
whole secret of life after death. It pivots on so many things—person
ality—condition of the physical and mental bodies. Carry on trying
though because you could soon be close to the secret. If you find it
no one will believe you anyway."

In many ways these statements turned out correct. In my short
and limited experience I have learned to be very careful when telling
people of certain psychic happenings.

Often I deliberately "play down" or completely leave out parts of
messages or happenings when relating them to friends. There appears
to be a limit to their readiness and willingness to accept them
completely.

I am quite sure that Myers is right: if I ever should discover what
causes the phenomena or the automatic writing, nobody will believe
me.

Often, when I have demonstrated one or the other phenomenon
for friends or strangers, they are perplexed and quite excited. After
an hour or so, having spent their time arguing and analysing what
they have just seen with their own eyes, they begin to doubt them
selves. Five minutes later they come up with all possible and ridicu
lous explanations; in the end they try to tell me that it just could
not be as they had thought before, because it goes against their will
to accept anything outside their personal experience and prejudice

Worthy of note are the different handwritings that the message
appear in. Some of them are in a style of handwriting that corres
ponds with that of the communicator whilst he or she was alive, and

المملكة العربية السعودية

لـت على شركات «لانغ» من منحدرات
وتشهد، بما في وبيروت والقرائي ، حرج

لا يـنـغ

جورج

The automatic scripts in Arabic were shown by Matthew's publishers to
Professor Suheil Bushrui of the American University of Beirut. The Professor
discussed these scripts with the publishers in London during his visit in 1973.
It appears that Matthew took down several scripts from different sources; they
range from the handwriting of a near illiterate writer to some calligraphical
artwork. In Professor Bushrui's opinion, these scripts could not have been
reproduced from memory. The narrative of the messages, however, provides
the greatest mystery of all the automatic writing received by Matthew. A
(architect/builder?) George Laing claims to have been murdered in Saudi
Arabia.

(Above) Some of the Arabic scripts taken down by Matthew. (Below) This
script which Professor Bushrui classified as belonging to a most literate
person, probably an academic, reads:

"Life consists of many (various) forces (powers) that live within us to the
end of time . . . of the body does not frighten us because we shall all come
together in the end. And death shall destroy all differences."

الحياة مكونة من قوى عديدة تمشى خلالنا الى نهاية الزمن
والنزعة الجسمية لا تخفنا لاننا كلنا سنجتمع فى النهاية
والموت سيحطم جميع الفوارق .

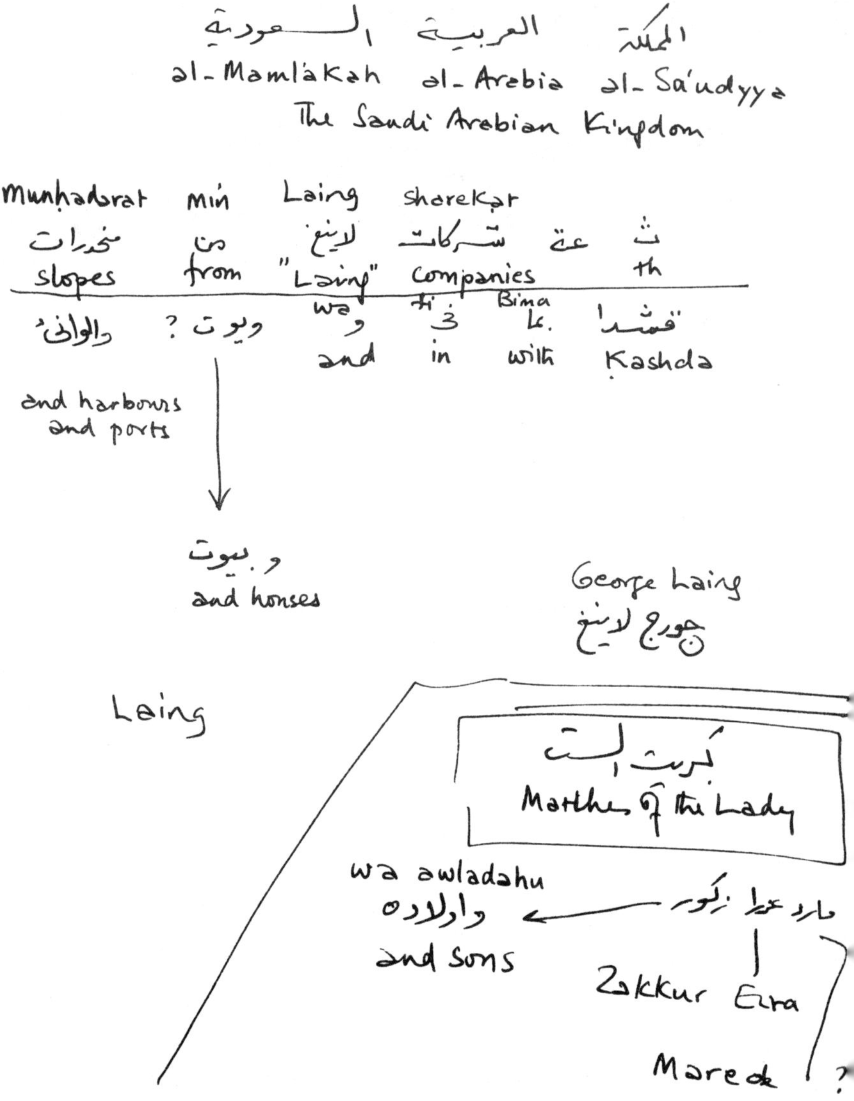

المملكة العربية السعودية

al-Mamlakah al-Arabia al-Sa'udyya
The Saudi Arabian Kingdom

Munhadrat min Laing shorekar
مخدرات من لينغ شركات ة عة
slopes from "Laing" companies th

قشدا ك. Bima ذ و wa
and in with Kashda

والوانئ ؟ وبيوت
and harbours
and ports

وبيوت
and horses

George Laing
جورج لينغ

Laing

أرشست لت
Marthes of the Lady

wa awladahu
واولاده
and sons

مارو عطا زكور
Zakkur Ezra

Marek ؟

Professor Suheil Bushrui prepared an analysis of the Arabic scripts. (Above)
This extract deals with the profession of George Laing. Several other names
are mentioned.

To everybody's surprise, Professor Bushrui identified the design at the bottom of this mythological drawing to be the name of George Laing.

some of them are in a style that is completely different. It seems though, that it is the content of the message rather than the style of handwriting that corroborates any possible evidence. Sometimes, however, the case is reversed and the handwriting appears to fit whilst the message makes apparently no sense at all. What is invariably correct is the signature on the message, which often is the same as the signature of the communicator when alive.

I have no explanation to offer nor can I comment on such messages which I wrote down automatically in foreign languages I don't know, or even in scripts which I would find difficult to reproduce if I tried copying them. The case of George Laing is particularly intriguing and is described in some detail later.

I know now that it was because of my automatic writing of several ancient and modern foreign scripts and messages, *The Psychic Researcher* showed interest in me. As the editor of that paper is also associated with my publishers, I faced probably more scepticism and tests than an author of a book would normally experience.

Whenever I was invited for yet another test or demonstration, those whom I had to meet and face were very rarely willing to take my word for anything. My most unnerving experience was being given a "third degree" interrogation by Major and Mrs. Cradock (better known as Fanny and Johnnie Cradock, the television gourmets).

For many months I thought Peter Bander, the editor of *The Psychic Researcher,* was positively out to expose me as some fraud. The news that he would finally decide whether or not my book would be published, worried me because not for six months did he indicate whether he really believed my story.

My natural shyness when meeting strangers always seemed to put me on the defensive; in time I have learned to accept and respect their caution and sometimes critical judgment. After all, at the age of seventeen and eighteen I am perhaps a rare specimen for so many psychic phenomena to happen to.

On September 26th, 1972, my grandfather had a heart attack and died straightaway; he was just about to get in his car and drive home when he collapsed in a car park.

Three months later many messages began to arrive, purporting to come from him, although I had not requested him to write. One of these scripts is very interesting:

"Matthew, I should not tell you this, but we feel that this could be useful for you, so I will tell you to the best of my ability. There are places that I am not clear about. It was beautiful, smooth, no fear and gentle. Much of this is going to be difficult to explain in writing.

"The last thing I remember was feeling very dizzy. I had a shocking headache. I think I clutched but caught hold of nothing, lost my balance and fell. Then a point I do not remember. I just do not know.

"Then I appeared to be *above* the ground. I saw a body *on* the ground and a man in a dark coat leaning over it. I then knew it must be my body. I hovered, I think, and watched as it lay motionless. All around was *quiet*. Next I saw a silvery cord from my body to the new entity. (Sorry about the writing. It is getting worse.) This cord extended from my shoulders, at the base of my head. Now there is another blank space. Looking up I saw a field of bright white light and faces I knew, but had long since lost. My new body was gently rising. I left my earth body down below, and I slowly lost sight of everything, as if I was *airborne*.

"I was completely relaxed, free, drifting all the time up. I lost sight of all on the ground. After a short journey I came to rest here, in peace, with friends, old relations, and quiet. I cannot put into words anything else in earthly terms for you.

"If we can continue to talk, I can give you more of a picture. Come back later. I can't go on now. A. G. Manning."

Whilst he was alive he knew of the psychic experiences our family had been through. He always appeared to be sceptical and not interested. And yet here was this message purporting to come from him. The signature was his, and the handwriting similar to his, but I cannot help thinking that the description he gives is rather contrived and a traditional view of death. This may be correct though and no one is in a position to judge. Even so, after a considerable amount of messages I received through automatic writing there were several interesting points he made. Some of the things he wrote were in keeping with his character as I knew it, some were alien to it. The senses, places, people and time scale he refers to are of interest.

At the beginning of the above message he writes, "but we feel that . . ." This rather implies that some sort of consultation has taken place concerning what he can tell me. He was not the type of person to make a grammatical mistake either, and there are several in the message. Then he says that, "much of this is going to be difficult to explain in writing". Later on he writes, "we can continue to talk". This suggests that he "sees" me as some kind of scribe, writing down what he "tells" me.

He describes "a short journey", which suggests that he has some sense of distance. Also he writes, "come back later" which hints that he is aware of some time scale.

This sense of time is again demonstrated with another message I received later. After his passing over, his wife suffered from a total nervous breakdown, from which, even today, two years later, she has not recovered, nor, according to medical opinion, is she likely to. At first my father did not know what to do about her, as all treatment seemed ineffective. He asked me to communicate with his father and seek advice from him. This I did and I was told by my grandfather that he could give no help. But, he said, if I gave him "time to think" he would see what he could do, and he asked for "twenty-four hours" to think about the problem. This was very much in keeping with his character: he would always try to have time to think about a problem, rather than give an immediate decision.

The next day he wrote:

"Matthew, since yesterday I have done some hard work which may help you. The doctor at N. (name given) is useless. Try:

The Phobic Trust
51, Northwood Avenue
Purley, Surrey.

They deal with this kind of thing and they might help you. Further than this I can think of no more. It may be worth a try, but you can never tell. I hope it will provide some sort of solution to a very worrying problem. Don't hesitate to ask me any more . . ."

The address given proved somewhat baffling. No one had heard of "The Phobic Trust". No one in our family knows Purley in Surrey.

Immediately we made enquiries about this address and discovered that it did exist, and that a small little-known registered charity known as "The Phobic Trust" operated from it. I was sure that my grandfather did not know this area, nor the "Phobic Trust". How he came to pass on its address was a mystery to me, until I received a letter from a lady who helps to run it.

She was, it transpired, associated with the Spiritualist movement, and in fact had some mediumistic powers herself. I have wondered whether my grandfather "picked her up" whilst she was practising her gifts, and then passed her address on through me.

When the next Grand National Race was due, I again asked Hayward Collins (a former professional punter), for the names of the horses that would win. (At no time have I put money on the horses he has advised.) Again I did not know the names of the horses, but he wrote:

"Grand National Race:
Put your money on Red Rum which will come in first, and on Crisp which will come second. The third place will be a tight spot so leave well alone. Take this advice though Matthew and you can only be right . . ."

Later in the day the results were announced. Red Rum finished first and Crisp finished second. Furthermore it was a photo-finish for the third place.

The following message I received at the same time and it was signed by Richard Stafford Cripps. It is another communication that arrived without any request from myself:

"I died in Switzerland on April 21, 1952. I am now restless. My body is at Sapperton. Where is Frith Hill? In the storm and uncertainty and fear the today permeate the world, set yourselves to become part of the hand God which stretches out to bring peace and patience and high standards of truth and justice to all peoples. Bless my body and allow mass. Here is Charles father now. I must go. Richard Cripps. (And then in block capitals), RICHARD STAF-FORD CRIPPS. 52."

Until after I received this message I had never heard of this name, and knew nothing of the man. However, research later showed that Richard Stafford Cripps, the post-war Labour minister died in Switzerland, on April 21st, 1952. When he died he was buried in a place called Sapperton in Gloucestershire, and he had lived at Frith Hill. His father was Charles Cripps.

I can only reiterate that the name was quite meaningless to me when I wrote the message down. Even afterwards, when my parents saw it, the thought never occurred to us that the writer had been a well known politician. Besides I was not even born when Richard Stafford Cripps died.

One communicator who has interested me is a gentleman named Thomas Penn, who appears to have been a doctor. He does not claim to cure, but seems able to diagnose illnesses. I cannot decide whether he was a doctor or an astrologer, but he is a person who consistently writes intelligently and constructively, and furthermore it would seem very accurately. He will only write diagnoses for me but does not reveal information concerning his previous life. Thomas Penn started writing one day when I was not really intent on writing automatically, but wondering about the ailing condition of my grandmother. My pen went across the paper:

"Please may I take the liberty of asking the birth date of your grandmother as it will help me. Do you consider the trouble mental or physical?"

I wrote down her date of birth and also that I believed her illness to be mental, whereupon the following message was written:

"Although the effects are great on Vuna Manning the cause is relatively simple. Basically her weak points are legs, ankles, thin bones, blood and circulation. Great care should be taken to keep the digestion working properly. She will be fit and well when living in a life of harmony; if worried her physical reactions will be quick.

"Her main problem at this time is an illness known as neurasthenia which at present she is recovering from. Accordingly she will suffer from loss of weight with poor digestion and irregular action of the bowels. Vague pains in any part of the body are complained of, and insomnia is common. She lacks self-confidence, cannot concentrate and worries over trifling matters. She may be querulous or given to brooding. Now, I can do little myself, but treatment will entail complete change, rest, and tonics are necessary. Cure may take several weeks.

"I cannot see clearly now, but she is suffering from an innocent tumour (neuromas tumour). This has been overlooked by the hospital and should be X-rayed. It is affecting her gliomas. Thomas Penn."

Perhaps this message is not a fair indicator of the accuracy of his information, since I already knew roughly what was wrong with my grandmother. Everything that Thomas Penn said was, or could be, wrong with my grandmother, in fact was proven to be so.

The medical terms used in the message point to the fact that the origin of this automatic writing is outside my own mind. I have no medical knowledge, and would not be competent to diagnose a condition with such phrases. (I still do not know what a "gliomas" is.)

Nobody had any knowledge or suspected that my grandmother might be suffering from a tumour, although when it was suggested to us by Penn, it sounded quite feasible. The hospital was persuaded by us to X-ray her head and to check whether there was anything physically wrong with her brain. After they had X-rayed her brain, they would not reveal whether in fact there was a tumour, nor did they deny it.

A point that struck me as odd was Thomas Penn's request for grandmother's birth date. It suggested something astrological to me.

A few days later a friend asked me to allow Thomas Penn to write a diagnosis on his ailing grandfather. Before he could say anymore I interrupted him, telling him not to tell me any more, except the name of the person in question, and his birthday. This he did, and Mr. Penn had this to say:

"Here we have an interesting problem. The weak points are, chest, epigastic region, stomach, digestive organs.

"He is liable to colds and rheumatism. He must be strongly advised to resist depressive moods and to fix his mind on the brighter aspects of life. He is greatly affected by environment. He has an iodine deficiency and should eat plenty of fish."

This message appeared to impress my friend as certain parts of it were correct and known to him. There were other parts that he was not certain about and would have to check up on.

Two days later he informed me that the entire diagnosis appeared to be correct; his mother corroborated this.

They also found out later that grandfather was to have an operation; however the hospital could not operate due to the fact that he had a serious iodine deficiency in his body, and he had to be put on a course of iodine tablets.

However, the next diagnosis that Thomas Penn made, was completely wrong. Again I was given just a name and a date of birth, and the following advice was given:

". . . her weak points are headaches, brain fatigue and neuralgia.

"These are symptoms of deep nervous troubles. Under pressure she could suffer insomnia, chronic catarrh. She is tense and ambitious which could lead to circulatory troubles caused by high blood pressure. She must retain a sense of balance . . ."

The person for whom I had done this writing told me it was completely wrong, but would not say why. He then told me that the birthday was anyhow two days later than he had told me, and so I again asked Thomas Penn for his diagnosis, giving him the patient's name and corrected birthday. This time he wrote:

"Her weak points are the nose, urinary and sex organs bladder and pelvic bones and generative powers. Moderation should be her strong point. She suffers it seems from inflammation of the joints which is chronic. She has an overgrowth of bone at the joints, creaking in the joint and limitation of movement. The trouble could stem from an abscess of the sinus, tonsil or tooth. Of these the first is most likely. Thomas Penn."

This new diagnosis was apparenty correct. I was told that the woman about whom this was written, was riddled with arthritis and crippled in a wheelchair, unable ot do anything for herself.

Other communications that I have received from Thomas Penn have been persistenty accurate. The only time he made mistakes was when he was given an incorrect birth date.

One very interesting diagnosis was received from Thomas Penn concerning a Mr. F. Smith. His son had asked me to find out what could be said about this person.

"Here we again have a relatively simple case. Weak points are legs, ankles, heart, blood and circulation.

"He is suffering from myrocorditis, the heart muscle being affected, which is resulting in auricular fibrillation in which the ventricles are beating irregularly, and his aurides are failing to contract and remain dilated and in a state of tremor.

"A quiet life and a non-stimulating diet are needed to cure. Something alien in his leg has given him trouble, but is safe now."

Rather than being merely a list of the patient's ailments, it explains what the heart trouble is and how it is caused.

However the most intriguing part of the message is contained in the ast line:

"Something alien in his leg has given trouble, but is safe now."

I had no knowledge of the medical condition of this gentleman or his past history. I was told later that whilst a young man, Mr. F. Smith had been the victim of a motor-cycle accident which had severely injured his leg. He had undergone an operation during which a metal pivot had been put in his leg. Initially this caused great discomfort, but this subsided after some time.

Thomas Penn is different in so many ways from the average communicator of messages. He is not petty, irrelevant or obstreperous as are so many of them. He does not ramble on, and what he writes is always positive and usually accurate. It is a contrast to the host of messages which warn that something "may happen", or that something else "may be wrong". Thomas Penn's descriptions are definite and decisive.

For reasons best known only to himself he prefers to retain a degree of anonymity. How the birth dates come into his prognostications, I do not know, but they appear to make a distinct difference to his diagnoses.

My automatic drawings have probably aroused the widest interest, and first brought me into contact with my publisher and *The Psychic Researcher*. Following the incident of the voice recordings on tape, I discussed the phenomenon with the author of *Carry on Talking*, Peter Bander. Following his invitation, I drove to Gerrards Cross and the sheer volume of drawings I took with me seemed to startle Mr. Bander and Mr. Smythe.

There and then I was interviewed for an article in the *Researcher*,

In June 1973, Matthew prepared himself for another automatic drawing. He was using a .2mm drawing nib and Indian ink; his hand suddenly moved with extreme vigour across the paper and the nib snapped off. He substituted the broken nib with a new one, .5mm thick; this one got bent after the first stroke. With a .8mm nib Matthew drew a sketch which was signed "Picasso".

"No other communicator tires me out as much as Picasso does," says Matthew. "After only a few minutes, the time it takes him to do one drawing, I feel worn out and cannot continue for at least twenty-four hours." The force which moves Matthew's hand during these automatic drawings is immeasurably stronger than that used by any other communicator.

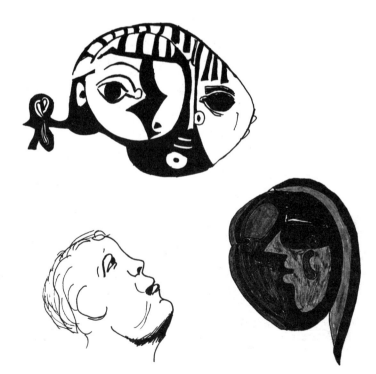

Matthew then placed his hand over a set of colour felt-pens and it appeared that his hand was guided first to the black pen; after a while, the movement on the paper stopped and Matthew's hand moved to the green colour. This process of selecting different colours continued with mauve, yellow, red and finally grey. When the picture was completed, his hand moved to black again and the signature Picasso appeared again. (opposite left)

After two sketches and one colour drawing, Matthew received no further automatic drawing from Picasso until February 1974; quite unexpectedly Matthew realised that his hand was again moved with excessive force, and colour felt-pens were chosen. Within minutes a picture appeared (opposite, right) which was signed Picasso.

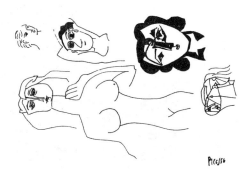

*Matthew received two drawings purported to come from **Aubrey Beardsley**;
neither drawing has particular artistic merit, but Matthew's experiences during
the execution is of interest: "I found myself making many mistakes; time and
time again, I felt frustration and irritation in my hand. Suddenly, something
which had just been drawn was covered over with black ink, usually leaving
a white space somewhere and something else, such as the small garden house
would appear. Everything appeared to be out of perspective. The final drawing was, in my opinion, a travesty of what I thought the picture would
represent when the drawing started. The horse-shoe design on the peacock's
tail is upside-down, the bird above the trees is completely wrong. Unlike all
other drawings, the peacock and the woman drawing took about six times as
long, and still appears incomplete. The drawing of John the Baptist's head
took under one hour, which compared with automatic work from other artists,
appeared to me an excessive amount of time."*

Anonymous

Anonymous

Anonymous

and the following extract which appeared in the July issue 1973, gives an accurate record of my own thoughts on the subject and reflects the impressions at the time:

"One of the communicating artists is the Elizabethan miniaturist Isaac Oliver, and among others who 'come through' are Albrecht Dürer, Thomas Bewick and Keble Martin.

"Asked how he knew it was those artists, Matthew said: 'I empty my mind as completely as possible and in that state I think of the person I am trying to contact—sending all my energy out to this person who then writes or draws through my hand.'

"Matthew himself claims no artistic ability yet the drawings which come through his hand are of a very high order. In the case of the Dürer drawings, art experts describe them as 'Very much in his style'.

"Asked if he could describe what extraordinary mental faculty he invoked to do the drawings, Matthew replied: 'I use what would be called kinetic energy associated, I think, with my subconscious. I think Dürer works through me so it would seem to prove survival, though I believe my subconscious plays a larger part in it.' "

A psychic researcher wrote to me after studying the drawings and observing me closely on many occasions:

"The physical instigator of these drawings is your hand, but further than that I cannot venture with a like degree of certainty. The inspiration—for want of a better word—seems to come from somewhere outside your consciousness. This conclusion is I feel substantiated by the quality of your drawings. Whilst some of these are reproductions of pieces previously done by the artist in his lifetime, several appear to never have been produced before . . ."

I have already mentioned that it was the sheer volume of automatic drawings which appeared to impress people most, and, I believe, the wide spectrum of artists who purport to execute these drawings through my hand. I deliberately tried to "tune in" with as many different artists as possible. I did not necessarily do so by asking a particular artist whose name I knew, and often I only discovered the identity when the signature "appeared".

Many of the drawings, however, remained incomplete and anonymous. Among those who "signed" are Albrecht Dürer, Rowlandson, Picasso, Bewick, Arthur Rackham, Leonardo da Vinci, Aubrey Beardsley, Paul Klee and Beatrix Potter.

I must here add two observations which, I believe, are important: I did quite frequently seek the co-operation of certain artists and, although I sincerely believe that the subsequent drawings originate from a source outside myself, I am sure that my subconscious may on occasions have caused me to embellish or add to some drawings This, however, I have never done voluntarily or consciously.

The other point is that while the work is unmistakably in the distinctive style of the artist who purports to execute the drawings, a certain proportion of the automatic drawings, usually those which I do first when an artist comes through, are merely reproductions or near copies of works executed by the artist when he was still alive. In most cases I am absolutely certain that I have never seen the original drawing before, and I am quite disappointed when it is explained to me by experts.

The only explanation I have is that the artist appears to be making a point of identifying himself beyond a shadow of doubt by reproducing something with which he is already known to be associated.

However, the majority of drawings I have received automatically, both signed and anonymous, complete and unfinished, appear to be "originals", never before drawn by the artist.

I use a draughtsman's pen with a continuous flow of Indian ink. I have found that this produces the best results. Using colour in any form, paint, felt-tip pens, coloured inks, etc., seems to baffle the artist; the colours get muddled up and the result is usually a very sub-standard work. Again, I have no explanation for this. All I have experienced points to the fact that mono-colour yields the best results.

The only artist to whom the use of colour presents no problems is the late Pablo Picasso. My experiences with him have been particularly interesting and different from those with other communicators. The first work from him came in July 1973, three months after he died. I had specifically asked Picasso to produce a drawing for me.

I had in my pen a nib with a width of 0.2 millimetres—the same thickness as I usually use for artists who produce fine work. Within seconds my hand was seized by what is best described as an extremely assertive force. So strong was it, that after a minute of very fast drawing the nib was snapped and rendered useless. I changed over to a thicker nib of 0.5 millimetres; this soon became bent, and it was not until I used a nib of 0.8 millimetres that the pen could take the strain of the force working on my hand. The drawing that I produced was unmistakably in Picasso's style; it was bold and strong.

I did this drawing with my customary black ink, although I had on my desk a packet of twenty-four coloured felt-tip pens. I found another clean sheet of drawing paper, and asking Picasso again to draw for me, I placed my hand over the range of colours. Out of the twenty-four colours, I was surprised to find that my hand was moved forcibly to the black pen. Rapidly a curious pattern of shapes and lines were placed on the paper, with the same assertive force as the previous drawing. What looked like a face was drawn with this black pen.

My hand suddenly moved to the green pen; it took it, and areas were coloured in with green ink. This procedure of colouring in particular areas and then switching to a different colour was repeated until they all made up a startling multi-coloured drawing of a face resembling some Egyptian king. After seven colours had been used, black, green, brown, purple, red, yellow, and grey, the picture was "signed".

It might well be asked, do I ask these artists questions in English or their own language? How do I ask Albrecht Dürer to draw through me, for example? He was not only German, but also died in 528, meaning that he spoke "old-German" rather than contemporary German. Leonardo da Vinci was Italian and died in 1529.

Whenever I do these automatic drawings, and want a particular artist, I just concentrate all my thoughts on the artist. I think of nothing else but the artist concerned. I am not in any trance state and perfectly aware of everything going on around me. However, I have been blind-folded on occasions and the results were often very sub-standard, which I find curious. Why, if these drawings are executed automatically, can I not produce good work without the use of my eyes? Logically it should make no difference and the communicators should still be able to write or draw. I have learned that psychic phenomena are neither logical nor predictable. Perhaps my situation can be likened to using a radio with no aerial. Seen in this light I could be regarded as a type of receiver that picks up communications from a transmitter. The fact that the person with whom I wish to communicate with does not speak English, is apparently no barrier. Even though I receive some messages in other languages than English, some foreign correspondents do write in English, or use an "interpreter" who acts as a third party to pass messages on to me.

Another interesting point about the drawings is the way that they always fill up the complete area of whatever size of paper I choose to use. If I have a sheet of paper two inches square it is filled up with no space to spare, as it is if I use a sheet of paper two feet square.

I have no guarantee that if I try to get a particular artist, I am in fact going to be able to communicate with him. This may account for a large number of "anonymous" drawings that I have done. When

I have tried to do a drawing with one particular person, someone else may intervene without my prior knowledge. He then draws and often does not sign his name. On other occasions I have received anonymous works because I have sat down with no particular name in my mind, having merely made myself receptive; this usually happens when I want to prevent an imminent spate of poltergeist activity. Somehow I feel a "build-up" of kinetic energy.

If I do no writing or drawing for two weeks or more, I become subjected to poltergeist activity. After I have been writing or drawing for much more than an hour, I begin to "run out" and feel tired. The messages become fainter until they fade away or become incomprehensible. It then takes some hours to "recharge".

One incident that occurred at just such a time is very interesting. At Christmas in 1972 I began a large drawing purporting to be by Isaac Oliver. I had asked him to draw for me Elizabeth I on a sheet of card 21 inches by 25 inches. He started in the centre of the sheet and worked out towards the edge, leaving not one square inch untouched with intricate detail.

I was still working on it, when I was asked if it could be used to illustrate a school magazine. I agreed, not knowing that I was only to be allowed a further seven days to complete nearly one-quarter of it. One Sunday afternoon a friend came to tell me that if it was to be included in the magazine he had to have it by the following morning. This was, I thought as good as impossible. With the space left that had to be filled in, I had not enough energy to complete it. However, at 7.30 that evening I began drawing again, knowing that if I ran out of energy I would be unable to complete the picture.

An hour later my energy was running low. By 9.00 nothing was coming from my hand. As far as I could see, I was unable to complete the drawing. It was at just about this time that another friend came in to see how I was getting on. I explained my predicament to him, and after some moments he said:

"I wonder whether it would make any difference if I collect up a group of people who will all concentrate on you, while you try and continue drawing. It is conceivable that we might achieve some sort of energy transference, so that you can use our energy to finish the drawing with."

We did as he suggested. He sat in another room, about ten yards away, with four other people, who all concentrated hard on me. I sat down again to draw and I concentrated on Isaac Oliver. Slowly my hand began to move and draw again. Initially I thought it was the remains of my energy producing the movement of my hand

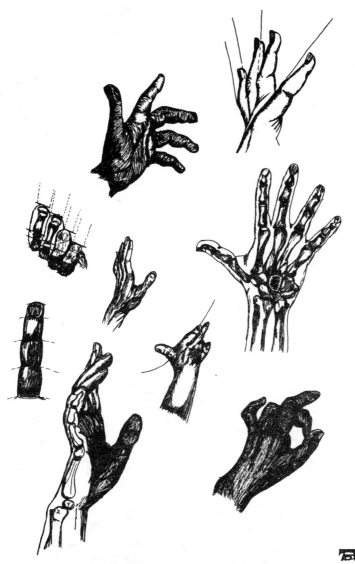

Matthew had reduced the poltergeist manifestations to a minimum by allowing himself to be used as a channel for automatic writing in June 1971. In November he found himself drawing sketches of a hand. In the course of one hour, a sheet of paper was filled with nine drawings, and the monogram *AD* appeared at the bottom.

MATTHAVS LANG VON WELLENBVRG
1522

BILIBALDI · PIRKEYMHERI
1503

During the following months, Matthew "received" about a dozen more drawings signed with the same initials. Several of them were obviously reproductions of drawings known to have been executed by Albrecht Dürer during his life; others were certainly in Dürer's style.

Many other artists appeared to use Matthew for automatic drawings but it appears that Dürer had attached himself more to the young man than others, (with the possible exception of Picasso who most forcefully took over Matthew's hand in June 1973).

128

More interesting is the large picture which Matthew drew after receiving an automatic message from Bishop Kephalas Nektarios who died in 1920: "I will get a spirit who is close to you who will do a drawing for me . . ." Nektarios wrote. Two days later, Matthew found himself drawing a picture. As usual, the drawing started in the middle of the paper and grew outwards in anti-clockwise movements. If this is a drawing of Nektarios, Albrecht Dürer sees this twentieth century Greek Orthodox bishop in a sixteenth century German setting. In fact, everything about this picture is Gothic, especially the monastery which, according to the messages by Nektarios, is the purpose of the communication. The initials AD are in the design.

On Saturday, 22nd March 1974, Matthew was asked if he could "link up wit
Dürer at will". At 12.05 midday, the young man suddenly began drawing. H
hand moved rapidly over the paper; his head kept swinging from left to righ
after each decisive move of the pen, the hand moved always back to th
centre of the paper where he had first started the drawing. At 12.18 a com
plete head and shoulders were completed; Matthew stopped and said the
"he" wanted another pen: "He feels that my ordinary fountain-pen is to
clumsy—he cannot get the details; he is not used to drawing with this thing.

Matthew was asked to try and continue; he tried, apparently without succes
The only lines which appeared look like an elaborate letter H on the le
shoulder. This would indicate that the communicator was not Dürer bi
somebody else. Matthew was unable to throw any light on the matter.

However, the energy seemed to be increasing, and I found no difficulties in drawing at my original speed. By 11.00 p.m. the picture was complete.

This incident did seem to have close connections with the method by which my younger sister can sometimes write automatically. She needs my presence as an additional external source of energy.

What of the contents and subjects of my automatic drawings?

Perhaps surprisingly, there are very few religious drawings among them. In fact, the only religious picture that I have produced, is a head of Christ purportedly by Leonardo da Vinci. Most drawings are of people, birds and animals; very few are of buildings.

Under the initials of Albrecht Dürer I produced a series of portraits, all of which are named after the subject. The names include "Matthaus Lang von Wellenburg", "Bilibaldi Pirkeymheri", "Hans Tucher", "Lucas van Leydon", and "Ulrich Stark". None of these names, with the exception of Lucas van Leydon, the engraver (contemporary of Dürer) were known to me. However, little research was needed to discover that Bilibaldi Pirkeymheri was a close friend and patron of Dürer.

I am sure that not all of these are originals; many of them are different versions or reproductions of previous works by the artist. However, there is still the question of how these pictures get through my hand onto the paper. I have never seen these pictures before, and I have really no ability at all to draw myself.

There are similar peculiarities in some drawings that Aubrey Beardsley has produced through my hand. I noticed it first on one fairly large drawing that obvious mistakes were being made. Sometimes an arm would be drawn quite wrongly and out of proportion, or a bird might be out of perspective; when this occurred, he appeared to black out and obliterate the area concerned, and turn it into something totally different, which instead of being left white would be black. I later learned that Beardsley, when alive, if he made a mistake, as he apparently did frequently, would stick over it another piece of paper. More than any other artist, Beardsley made many mistakes when drawing through me, but instead of covering them over with paper, which obviously he could not do, he inked over them and changed them into something different. He has on occasions made mistakes and not bothered to correct them; on one drawing for example, a peacock has been drawn with the design on the tail the wrong way round.

Most remarkable about these drawings is the speed with which they are drawn. They are usually started in the middle of the paper and then worked out towards the perimeter. They are always drawn

Le renard prêche aux poulets et quand on parle du loup, on en voit la queue.
Il n'est point de roses sans épines. Goya.

On two occasions, Matthew refused to continue with a drawing. In October 1973 a picture emerged which made him physically ill. The distorted and mutilated figure of a man was drawn with a nightmarish owl on his shoulders. Matthew tried to stop several times but somehow felt compelled to continue. The drawing is poor and vulgar. When Matthew finally shook himself out of the compulsion to draw, the pen moved to the top of the sheet and writing appeared in French: "one cannot have roses without thorns. Goya."

The second occasion when Matthew refused to continue a drawing was when a hanged man emerged. This time he stopped after a few minutes. Again, the pen moved to an empty space and writing appeared.

straight onto the paper in ink with no preliminary work or pencil outlines. Mistakes hardly ever occur, although on a few of the drawings are some technical faults in perspective or shading.

Although I might spend one or two hours to produce a drawing, it would normally take an artist perhaps six or eight hours to draw the same picture. I think this alacrity can be accounted for by the fact that the drawings are being produced with little or no forethought or planning.

Whilst I was at school there was frequently a strong temptation to get "someone else" to do some of my work in my examinations; in fact it was frequently suggested that I do this by my fellow students. When I happened to get good marks for a piece of work, I was accused of having summoned outside help! However, I never used spiritual intervention to help me with my work, until one morning when I decided that I would try it just to see whether it did in fact work. The effects were amusing.

We had been set an English test-essay on Wordsworth's poetry, and I had done no revision for it. When I saw the title of the essay I was completely at a loss for anything to write. It was rather cheering to see that the person sitting next to me knew nothing either.

I began writing an introductory paragraph in my normal handwriting, and having waffled for several lines, could think of no more. It was then that I was struck by the idea of asking an outside source for help, and Keats was the first person to come to mind. I did know that he had had a good knowledge of Wordsworth's poetry as he had written a work on that subject.

And so underneath what I had already written myself, I asked Keats for some help, reading the title several times over in my mind.

I was surprised when eight lines of writing appeared in a handwriting that was totally different to my own. What was written was intelligent and relevant to the title, and gave me enough ideas to continue for a couple of paragraphs under my own steam. After that I had again to call on the helpful Mr. Keats for some more ideas. He obliged and wrote another paragraph, after which I wrote some more myself.

At this point my next-door neighbour happened to glance over at me and saw what was written on my paper. He immediately realised what I was doing and shouted loudly about inequality and unfairness. I just grinned at him and continued writing. When I ran out of material again, Keats wrote further notes for me on a seperate scrap of paper, reminding me of things that I would have forgotten otherwise.

After the lesson I was questioned by my curious and baffled friends, who wanted to know what I had done and written. I had no option but to admit that the essay was not all my own work!

When the essay had been marked it was handed back to me. Although the master who had marked it said nothing about the two different handwritings, I noted that all the "ticks" had been placed in the margin next to what Keats had written.

That was the only time when I did use outside help for my school work, but it was an interesting and "rewarding" experiment.

In a school as large as mine, different stories and rumours are bound to circulate. Some masters and pupils were wary of me. Some resented "this nonsense", others talked about "madness" or my "desire to attract attention". There were also a good many who were frightened of me, and few were keen to get on the wrong side of me or openly annoy me.

The consequences of someone annoying me were sometimes amusing, looking at it in retrospect. The "offender" would invariably suffer some breakage or poltergeist phenomenon. On five occasions when I was more than usually angered by someone's snide comments, light bulbs have left their sockets and smashed on the floor near them, or pools of water materialized on the floor.

One day I smelled something burning as I sat reading and thought it was a smell drifting in from outside. However, as it grew stronger I realised that there was something burning near me. When I put down my book and jumped up, the rush matting was smouldering across an area of six inches at my feet. Smoke was spiralling upwards and small flames were spreading. It was fortunate that I caught the fire at this stage; if it had been left much longer it would quickly have spread.

I never discovered the cause of this incident. There were no wires or pipes of any description near the spot where the mat had ignited, and I do not smoke.

Corresponding with the incidents that have occurred occasionally when I am annoyed, are a number of poltergeist movements that have taken place many miles from where I was at the time. These seem to have happened at times when I was trying to contact a friend.

The first example of this was demonstrated when the poltergeist activity raged around me at school and I had been in fairly close contact with my family. It happened on a Saturday night, following a decision by the Headmaster to ask me to leave the school on the next day.

My sister, awoke in the early hours of the morning for apparently no reason, to find her pillow had vanished. Putting on the light she got out of bed and found it in the opposite corner of the room. Then she found that her alarm-clock was no longer by the side of her bed; this she found *under* her bed.

I had, of course, been very worried that night and thought about my family throughout the night. Somehow I wished I could let them know that it was not my fault that I was to be sent home from school.

I wished even that my sister should experience those happenings so that my parents could not blame me alone. I felt miserable and very alone in my plight.

By the time the Matron of my house at school left to look after her father who had fallen ill, we had become very friendly. I continued to write to her and went to see her several times. On three occasions, objects were found to have moved in her home, after I had been trying to contact her unsuccessfully by telephone. At that time a relative was living with her who also witnessed these events. On one occasion when I decided to telephone her, he answered the call. As soon as I had given my name, he said:

"You've been trying to get her before, haven't you? Last night a lamp fell over in her sitting-room, and this morning a chair had been put against my door from the inside. I am here alone—she will not be back until this afternoon."

I had tried the previous night and earlier in the morning to telephone her, but there had been no reply. Once when this occurred she knew that I was trying to contact her and she then proceeded to telephone me.

"Do you know anyone called George Laing? Have you ever received an automatic message from him? Do you know anything about this man or is that name known to your father?"

"No, I don't recall any name like that. I don't know anybody with that name. Why?" I asked my publishers over the telephone. I was mystified.

"We have one of your messages here and a George Laing appears to be connected with it," I was told.

I could not remember having received a message from anyone called George Laing. The name meant nothing to me.

Later it transpired that my publishers had sent two sheets of my automatic messages in Arabic to Professor S. Bushrui at the American University of Beirut.

The professor had just visited my publisher and brought back with him the translations of the messages.

When he translated them, several odd but interesting facts emerged. The content of the messages made apparently little sense, except for one; also, various parts were written in different and distinct handwritings that ranged from a well-educated and literate hand to a style that would probably be written by an uneducated man. One person could not have written them all. Professor Bushrui graded each message according to the script from one to ten and on the content. He also drew up a graph, showing the type of Arabic Scripts, and indicating that the contents of the sentences corresponded in quality with the literate or illiterate handwriting.

There was, however, one message he found out of character. In decorative and artful lettering it said, "Kingdom of Saudi Arabia". Professor Bushrui was suspicious because these words appeared on Saudi Arabian banknotes and on Royal or governmental letter-headings. The professor suggested I could have seen this and either consciously or sub-consciously copied it. The script was perfect as far as the calligraphy was concerned; one of the publishers tried to copy what I had written. He could reproduce the Arabic script, but only very slowly and not perfectly. Even if I had copied "Kingdom of Saudi Arabia" from somewhere, the professor felt that it did not account for the coherent sentences that were included in some of the other messages.

It was at this stage that I had the telephone call and was asked about George Laing. They took great care not to say anything else to me, but merely that they were interested in a certain George Laing who was connected with one of my automatic writings; they did not even tell me that this name was connected with an Arabic script.

As I knew no such person I decided to see if I could find out anything about this George Laing through my automatic writing.

No writing appeared, however, when I tried to communicate with George Laing. Still curious to find out what the mystery was, I asked anyone for information concerning this George Laing. Within thirty seconds my hand began to move and the following message resulted:

"George Laing asks me to tell you that he was murdered by a servant of the king's household and not many know because the police were no good and his body was buried on the slopes. He wants to know why he died when he was trying to help to build houses and develop the ports. He was hit on the head and died in the Kingdom of Saudi Arabia. Poor George, how is his building?

Carry him through and hoist the flag. We are only simple because you are stupid and we have many barriers to cross.

Monique Vanderhout."

I put the message in the post and sent it to my publishers. I was still not put in the picture, and all I knew was what was contained in the message from Monique Vanderhout; this did not strike me as being particularly important and relevant.

Peter Bander telephoned two days later:

"This message is just too good to be true. In fact its so remarkable that I can't help being suspicious of it. It's like finding a murdered man and discovering that the picture of his murderer is still visible in his eyes," he told me over the telephone.

I was still puzzled why this message should have caused such an impression and asked it if it mattered if someone called George Laing had been murdered. Only now did I receive some explanation, but only a very cautious one.

Professor Bushrui had come across a passage that struck him as odd. It was on the script with the heading "The Kingdom of Saudi Arabia". What followed was a series of disconnected words that did not make up a coherent sentence. These words, when translated into English, were, "Kingdom of Saudi Arabia", "slopes", "build houses", "ports", "buildings", "hiding", "rocks", "rubble". In two places the name George Laing appeared in Arabic script.

Perhaps no one would have taken any further notice of this fragmented message, had it not been for one of my drawings that Professor Bushrui saw. It was a rather striking picture of a beautifully drawn eagle carrying Sinbad in its talons. In one corner of this drawing was what looked to me an Eastern signature. As the artist of this picture was obviously Eastern, judging by the style of the drawing, I had assumed that this was his signature.

However, it was immediately recognised as another piece of Arabic by Professor Bushrui. The signature was in fact a design that incorporated the name George Laing.

By now it was evident to me that somebody called George Laing was trying to get a message through to me. If this was the case, there were many questions arising from this.

Why was such a typically British name, George Laing, appearing in Arabic scripts? If he was so desperate to communicate, what was his problem? Why were his messages so fragmented and what was the relevance of "The Kingdom of Saudi Arabia"? It was for these reasons that I had been asked what I knew about George Laing.

When I produced the message from Monique Vanderhout all the

138

pieces of the jigsaw suddenly fell together, and the fragments in Arabic became relevant and meaningful, especially those which had earlier been discarded by Professor Bushrui.

A George Laing had obviously been murdered whilst working in Saudi Arabia. The script from Monique Vanderhout gave all the details more coherently.

The amazing thing about her message was the fact that it contained all the words that were in George Laing's Arabic message. At no time did I have any idea of the content of the Arabic script when I asked for "assistance".

Obviously, the next thing to do was to make enquiries about this George Laing, who was evidently unaccounted for and missing, having been quietly murdered and disposed of in Saudi Arabia.

I therefore set about asking Monique Vanderhout if she could tell me when George Laing had died. She wrote:

"Here is poor Monique who was killed by her loving husband's bullets, to tell you that George Laing joined us in 1943. This is odd, why must you put us off with the radio. It makes it so difficult for us in a small space . . . Monique Vanderhout."

It was interesting that Monique noted that I was automatically writing in a small room with a radio on.

Little else was discovered about George Laing, apart from the name of a man who was said to have murdered him and where. I also managed to draw a picture of him (automatically). When he was murdered at Sakaka by a "servant called N. (name given)", there must have been quite a struggle, if George Laing died only from a blow on the head, because the drawing of him revealed a large muscular man who would have been a good match for anybody.

I have often been asked whether I hear or see anything while I do automatic writing. Mediums seem to receive strong impressions concerning their communicators, or even see them. However, I get no such impressions, although I can gauge the strength of the person by the pressure applied to the paper by my hand.

Recently I took part in a long-range extra-sensory perception test with Dr. George Owen in Toronto, Canda. Dr. Owen had invited several people in Britain, America, and Canada to participate in a series of experiments concerned with E.S.P. He was interested to discover whether distance played any part in determining the strength of it, and how accurate it was. He sent out to the participants a selection of six lists: the first list comprised five objects, the second list was of five names, the third list was made up of the symbols of a pack of zener cards, the fourth was a list of five colours, the fifth list was one of the subjects of five picture postcards, and on the sixth list we were given the numbers from o to 999. Then in the basement of his home in Toronto he placed one item from each of the six lists. Only he knew what these six objects were. It was the task of the participants to guess which articles were placed in the cellar.

After everyone had done this and sent their guesses to him he wrote to me saying:

"Your result on the first round was extremely good. The actual target selection was:

			Matthew	Probabilities
A cracker biscuit	...	...	Correct	1/5
Edgar	...	...	Vincent	—
742	...	...	749	1/9 x 1/10
Square	...	...	Waves	—
Motor vehicle	...	...	Mountain	—

"Your probability of getting so much right by chance was:

1 in 5 x 9 x 10 = 1 in 450.

"Your impression of our house is perfectly accurate as far as i goes."

Personally I did not feel that these results were particularly re markable, but obviously the chances of guessing that much correctly were 1 in 450, according to Dr. Owen's statistics. However, while doing this experiment I did also receive an impression of his house which I have never seen and which he has not described to me.

Not being in a position to put forward satisfactory explanation for what I have described I have left that task to those more qualified than myself.

In his work "Can we explain the Poltergeist?" Dr. George Owen wrote:

". . . the amounts of energy required are not large in relation to the physiological supply normally available even in a small child. A four-stone child raising itself through five feet in ten seconds by running up a short flight of stairs does 280 foot-pounds of work and is developing power at the rate of twenty-eight foot-pounds per second. If paranormally the child raised a four-stone weight through five feet in ten seconds (and this would be quite a spectacular feat for the average poltergeist), the energy and power supply would be just the same as those provided physiologically in running upstairs Thus ordinary sources of physiological energy are quite adequate even for the most striking achievements in poltergeist mechanics and there is no need to look to superabundant vitality as a necessary factor."

CHAPTER VII

IN THE latter months of 1973 Uri Geller arrived in Britain and caused a blaze of publicity. He succeeded, I think, in convincing a large proportion of the British public with his astounding demonstrations of psychokinesis and mind-reading.

After he had demonstrated his talents on a "David Dimbleby Talk-in", televised by the BBC during December 1973, several magicians claimed that they could reproduce any of Geller's feats, using no paranormal powers; he was, they said, merely an accomplished magician. There can be little doubt that Geller's critics were largely instrumental in causing many of Uri's would-be followers to think twice about what they had seen. The argument that began to ferment was based on one issue: is Geller a psychic, verifiable under laboratory conditions or merely an illusionist and magician.

After watching the documentary "Uri Geller: Is Seeing Believing?" televised by ITV in January 1974, I was somewhat distracted by the opposing points of view presented in the programme. The whole film had an air of scepticism about it which came out strongly in the fervently maintained assertion of one of the cameramen who claimed that he had witnessed Geller acting fraudulently. He said that whilst Uri had been attempting to discover telepathically which of ten identical tins contained a concealed object, Geller had moved his leg; this, claimed the cameraman, would cause the tin, containing the object, to remain stationary while the empty tins would move. With equal conviction another witness claimed that Geller had never moved his leg. Uri himself countered that people saw what they wanted to see.

My parents had watched this programme with me, and when it finished it was my mother who asked me to try if I could bend metal objects. I told her that I would not succeed but took a stainless steel spoon on which to experiment, more to please her than for any other reason.

I sat rubbing it gently and urging it mentally to bend. After ten minutes the spoon was still in its original shape and was evidently not being affected by my invocations. After another ten minutes when my father entered the room, I showed him the spoon and explained that nothing was happening.

His entry into the room had distracted my concentration and my concentration was diverted from the spoon as soon as I began talking to him. At that moment I felt something happening to the handle of the spoon. Somehow the handle was no longer so rigid. On closer inspection the spoon had an obvious bend in its handle.

Following this it continued to droop quite rapidly until it resembled the shape of a hairpin.

Even now I was dubious about the bent spoon: I really thought that inadvertently I must have bent it physically. My parents, who strangely enough were not very surprised at this achievement, thought later that night of a simple method of proving whether or not I had bent the spoon and a fork by force. My father produced a six-inch nail of a quarter-inch diameter made of galvanised steel. We thought that if I managed to bend this, I must be utilising a paranormal source of energy. Not believing that the nail would actually bend unless I physically applied pressure to it, I took it in my hands and found that I was quite incapable of bending it with my fingers, nor could I bend it by placing it in a vice and exerting manual pressure on it.

I tried in vain for fifteen minutes to bend the nail by paranormal means. When I realised that I was getting very tired, I gave up.

I decided to go to bed and, looking at the pendant watch that I wear around my neck, I saw to my surprise that the large minute hand was twisted towards the glass of the watch. This convinced me that I had been using a psychokinetic force earlier. The watch had not been opened for some time and the hands had always been quite straight.

As I lifted the watch on its chain over my head, the chain appeared to break; I always remove my watch by this method when I take it off, rather than undo the clasp. The break in the chain may be merely a coincidence.

As an interesting experiment I decided to sleep with the six inch nail under my pillow, merely to see whether anything would happen to it during the night.

At eight o'clock the next morning there was a bend of about thirty degrees in the steel nail.

Later that morning I took another spoon. My mother was just clearing up in the kitchen and called out, "Wait a moment, don't start yet."

"Don't worry," I assured her, "I can't do anything in such a short time."

To my surprise and my mother's annoyance, within seconds, the handle of the spoon began to bend, even though I had merely held the object and thought about bending it. It bent to the shape of a

In January 1974, Matthew watched Uri Geller bending objects on a television programme. This was the first time that he had seen Uri Geller performing. He was challenged to try a similar experiment and succeeded against his own expectations. Several experiments were made during which metal objects were bent by no apparent physical force. On 8th March 1974, in the presence of a scientist, Mr. Graham Hodgetts of Cambridge, and other witnesses, a teaspoon bent without having been touched by Matthew. He had held his hands about six inches away from the spoon while concentrating. Two prongs fell off a fork while Matthew held the handle in his hand, and two other prongs "collapsed". On Monday, 4th February, Matthew was in the company of his publishers visiting Archbishop Athenagoras. Again, while holding the handle of a fork, one of the prongs curled downwards. On 26th February, the Vicar of Linton visited Queen's House; Matthew was asked to hold a fork in his hands and attempt an experiment. The handle bent and two prongs curled up. All witnesses testify that Matthew did not exert any physical force, and they added that the fork used could not have been bent physically unless it were put into a vice.

On 7th March, The Chancellor of Corpus Christi College, Cambridge, The Rev. E. Garth Moore, President of the Churches Fellowship for Psychical and Spiritual Studies, examined a four-inch steel nail and stated that it was absolutely straight and that it could not be bent by physical force without the help of tools. After Matthew had held the nail for ten minutes in his hand, the Chancellor agreed that the nail had been bent.

Matthew made the following observations: he cannot bend an object entirely at will; strong concentration, especially if he finds himself under pressure from observers, yields little or no result. As soon as the concentration is slightly broken, through somebody talking about another subject, the metal object seems to bend almost immediately.

hairpin, as had the spoon the night before. In similar fashion, a fork and a teaspoon buckled. The knife was apparently inpervious to my thoughts because it remained quite rigid.

Beginning to clear away the breakfast table, my mother called me in. The stainless steel teaspoon with which I had been eating a grapefruit, had a conspicuous bend in its handle.

Apart from one other curious incident I did not succeed in bending any other metal objects that day.

We have an aluminium clothes-airer which is designed to allow damp clothes to be hung over the metal arms, each of which is two feet long. The metal is particularly tough and resilient in order to bear the weight of a load of wet or damp clothes. As the airer is only screwed to a wall, it is impossible to bend any of the metal arms without wrenching the entire appliance from the wall.

During the course of the morning I put on the dryer a small wet muslin bag through which I had been straining fruit. I found the bag lying on the floor beneath the appliance when I looked at it an hour later, and found the arm on which I had hung my bag drooping like a plant.

It was impossible to bend the arm back in its proper position.

Two days later I found some old silver spoons that once belonged to my grandmother and I decided to experiment with them.

Strangely enough, I found them much harder to bend than the stainless steel cutlery. Although I could have easily bent them physically, they required a far longer period of time of concentrated effort (thirty minutes as compared to ten or fifteen) before they showed the slightest sign of bending. They also only bent to a far shallower angle than the steel spoons. For this I have no explanation, other than suggesting that certain metals, or alloys, are easier to work with.

While I had had a silver spoon in my hands I saw a metal comb lying on a window sill about eight feet away from me. I did not touch the comb at all and I was astonished to notice that the comb was also bending.

I believe that this metal bending phenomenon is just mind over matter and does not in any way involve the spirits of departed persons; perhaps in my case (I don't think this applies to Uri Geller), it is perhaps possible to regard the force as being a controlled poltergeist energy.

The *Sunday Times* (2nd December, 1973) published an article about the abilities of Uri Geller. The author, a scientist, said:

"At one extreme Uri Geller could simply be exposed as a fraud. At the other, missiles could be knocked out of the sky by mind power alone. But these are not the only ways in which the affair can develop. There is a third altogether more boring possibility. The Geller Effect could turn out to be real, but rare and useless, except for doing tricks. It could become a kind of scientific backwater, useless in practical terms, and incomprehensible theoretically, and therefore disliked. I have a nasty feeling that is the way it is going to turn out."

Although the article referred to Uri Geller only, I believe it is applicable to those who, like myself, have similar experiences, abilities or whatever people may call it.

Any notions of this power "being useless, except for doing tricks" I don't accept. It may at present be "incomprehensive theoretically" but that will hopefully be resolved in the future.

Perhaps this record of my own experiences will help a little.

If the day should come that my psychic abilities have left me, I shall be the first to say so. There is a novelty value to each and every phenomenon, but after a while it becomes rather boring and annoying, especially to the person who has to live with them whether he likes it or not.

Those interested in learning more about Matthew are advised to read his later books. *In the Minds of Millions* (1977) is out of print, as is his *Guide to Self-Healing* (1989), but they should both be obtainable through your local public library.

A paperback edition of *The Strangers*, originally published in 1978, is being published by this company in 1995. His next book, *No Faith Required*, is also being published this year.

Matthew devotes all his time to healing. His address, if you want to get in touch with him, is

P.O. Box 100
Bury St Edmunds
Suffolk IP29 4DE
or you can send a fax to him at 01284 830228.

He has prepared over thirty cassettes for sufferers, the subjects covered including allergies, blood pressure, cancer, depression, eyesight, insomnia, living with grief, multiple schlerosis, and pain. A complete list of cassettes is available on request from The Rock Warehouse Ltd., P.O.Box 602, Ilford, Essex, IG3 8EP (phone: 0181 597 9999).

Professor Brian Josephson, Trinity College Cambridge, Nobel Prize Winner in Physics, was one of the twenty-one scientists who examined Matthew's extraordinary psychic gifts in Toronto. A re-examination of "reality" and "non-reality" was asked for by Prof. Josephson because the definitions applied to "non-reality" have to be revised after the results obtained during the Toronto experiments.

Dr. Karlis Osis, Director of the American Society for Psychical Research, found the happenings he witnessed quite staggering. There appeared to be no limit to Matthew's gifts, and what should have been hours of rest were usually taken up with further experiments.

APPENDIX I

THE CASE OF
BISHOP KEPHALAS NEKTARIOS

A REPORT BY PETER BANDER,
EDITOR OF
"THE PSYCHIC RESEARCHER"

DURING the latter part of 1973, I was asked by His Eminence Archbishop Athenagoras, Greek Orthodox Metropolitan of Great Britain, to examine and assess some unusual phenomena concerning a member of his Church, Mrs. C. Katsikides of Wandsworth, and the apparent communication between her and the late Bishop Nektarios who had died in 1920.

To my surprise I received a telephone call from Matthew Manning on Monday, 12 November during which he told me that he had received an automatic message, signed by the said Nektarios. This message was forwarded to me by post:

> *and I shall continue to appear on my feast day, each November 9 until we have a monastery to twin the monastery of Aegina. At Aegina will much take place in new years. Here will one day appear our Blessed Lady. We must erect a monument to her: the site will be marked by her coming. I shall explain more soon. I have much to tell but it is so difficult. It is Aegina that is necessary for the monastery. Please go there.*
>
> Kephalas Nektarios†
1920

On 13, 22 and 29 November, Matthew sent me further automatic writings purporting to come from Nektarios.

13 November:

> *and my advice now is to go to Zoë. There you will receive help and advice and backing. Zoë will provide funds. Still go to Hieronymos—he is safe.*
>
> Kephalas Nektarios†

22 November:

> *when so many people are going to Aegina each year to see my tomb make collections to build my monastery. We must have*

this built here in England. Raise the money. Aegina needs a couple and when you see Our Blessed Lady that is where must be the site. Just allow time to reveal my intentions. I will guide you all. When you all meet—there will be five of you I will make all clear. Just 8000 in Aegina—they can start you on your way. Go Ascetic.

Kephalas Nektarios†

29 November:

I am afraid that when the time arrives for the monastery to be built there will be displeasure from Chrysostomos and Athens. Our Blessed Lady is the sign and Hieronymos will support you throughout. Go to him for help and say I sent you. He will understand. Beware of Turkey. This monastery will further the unity between Churches of Rome and the Orthodoxy. There the Patriarch will be of help.

Kephalas Nektarios†

These messages contained several points which I did not understand. First, I wanted to know who *Kephalas* was; secondly, I had been under the impression that Nektarios's feast day was on 11 November; the references to Aegina, Zoë, Hieronymos and Chrysostomos needed clarification. From Archbishop Athenagoras I received this information. *Kephalas* was the surname of Bishop Nektarios; the feast day was, in fact, 9 November; Aegina was the place where Nektarios had worked and was buried; Zoë is an organisation of Greek Orthodox priests and theologians; Chrysostomos—remains somewhat of a mystery and Hieronymos is the deposed Archbishop of Athens.

I had almost forgotten these messages, when Matthew arrived at my office on Monday, 4 February '74, and showed me yet another message. Matthew asked whether he could go to Battersea but I advised him against it because I felt uneasy about two separate investigations getting muddled up. Instead I took Matthew with me to visit Archbishop Athenagoras; the message which the Archbishop studied, received a guarded reception:

and still we do nothing. Why? Follow:

I   My previous instructions. Aegina.
II   You go to Battersea where will I deliver further message.
III   Go to the Rhizarion College where you will collect more funds. Money is what we need for my monastery. All of you together must discuss and act as a unified whole. Do not delay

150

"I have read the messages which are said to have been received from Kephalas Nektarios to Mr. Matthew Manning and I am indeed puzzled. I know that the organisations and the names mentioned therein are real.

"As to the contemplated Monastery of St. Nektarios here in England to be a parallel with the Monastery which is flourishing in Aegina, I hope and pray that this will be realised, and that through it the Christian peoples of the West and of the East will have a centre of prayer and Christian activity for the rapprochement of the Churches."

Athenagoras, Archbishop of Thyateira and Great Britain

In November 1973 Matthew Manning received the first of a series of automatic messages from Bishop Kephalas Nektarios who died in 1920. In March 1974 Matthew was shown two photographs of the late bishop; "Nektarios is so impatient and quite forceful," Matthew explains, "he suddenly 'comes through' —and my hand just moves across the paper and takes down his message." The Nektarios-case is particularly interesting because of cross references to psychic phenomena elsewhere.

*further now please. Roch is with you two now. His feast day is
your day of birth son. Go on Tuesday to the Church.*
My Blessings be with you
Kephalas Nektarios†

On 1 March '74, I wrote to Archbishop Athenagoras the following
letter:
"Nektarios is certainly a prolific 'writer'; Matthew telephoned
me yesterday and I received yet another 'message' from him in
today's mail.

I admit to being baffled: your name appears and that of two
other persons whom I don't know and have never heard of.

As you see, Nektarios states that these two gentlemen, Eusebius Matthopoulos and Makrakis, are with him. From this I
conclude that they are no longer on this earth. Also, he main-
tains that you know Matthopoulos.

Here, first of all, is the message:

*'Here again am I. Let us use foresight now. To help me I have
with me Eusebius Matthopoulos and Makrakis. They too want
the monastery and at Zoë Matthopoulos will be known, seen
and loved. Athenagoras can tell you about Matthopoulos. We
are three united by one aim.*
*Makrakis is sure that much of the answer will be found in the
Book of Revelation but cannot agree with the Synod. He says
this will you find useful. Take it.*
*I shall carry through on April 14 if it is permitted and then
Our Blessed Lady will show at the temple. Please raise money.
I can do no more than instruct. I need apostles.*
Kephalas Nektarios†
1920'

Apart from my obvious question about the names mentioned
in this message, I think I must ask an even more important
question: what is your verdict on the origin, purpose and
genuineness of these 'letters' signed by †Kephalas Nektarios?

Does Your Eminence feel that action should be taken with
regard to the requests expressed, and if so, what should be done?"

On the same day, the Archbishop had posted a letter to me. At
this point I consulted the Religious Editor of *The Psychic Researcher*, the Rev. David Kennedy (Church of Scotland) and submitted to him the entire material concerning the Nektarios case:

On 27 February '74, His Eminence Archbishop Athenagoras
returned from his visit to Athens where he had attended a

Synod of Metropolitans of the Greek Orthodox Church. Among his mail he found a letter dated 29 January 1974 from Mrs. Olof Ericson, wife of the Consul General of Greece in Gothenburg, Sweden.

His Eminence sent me a photocopy of the letter which takes up almost two foolscap pages of typewritten matter. Mrs. Ericson reminds the Archbishop of their previous meeting in Sweden and apologises for taking his time, reading the long letter. The cause for writing to him was a dream or vision she had encountered the previous night which contained a direct 'message' for Athenagoras.

There appears to be some confusion as to *who* spoke in her vision; first, Mrs. Ericson gives a verbatim quote she received: "In the right time I will tell you, Athenagoras, how to do!" —and she then continues her narrative:

"I went away to a big house, built with red bricks. A few steps from the street there was a big open door and I looked into a very big room through a vaulted passage. There were many people streaming to you, and I did not like to disturb you.

"Then I saw a very sweet-looking lady among all the bearded men in monk habits. She saw me and asked what I wanted. Then she told you to come out to me so that I could give you the message 'In the right time, I will tell you how to do'."

Without wishing to over-state a case which, on serious examination may simply turn out to be a string of coincidences, Mrs. Ericson's dream is very similar to the visions by Mrs. C. Katsikides in Battersea, London, although the latter gives more detailed explanations and is absolutely certain about this building being a monastery. If we add to these two independent cases the messages received for Archbishop Athenagoras through Matthew's automatic writing, all of which contain references to a monastery to be built, I wonder at what point we ought to (if at all) take a positive or even active lead in our paper. So far, I have restricted our reporting to three articles on Matthew (without mentioning those messages to Athenagoras); one article on Mrs. Katsikides (The Apprentice Saint of Battersea), which certainly was cautious and strictly non-committal, and one quote from Athenagoras in that article, giving full protection to Mrs. Katsikides.

You will appreciate that we must be absolutely certain before acting. Of the three people involved, Matthew's 'evidence' is the most outstanding, at least in my opinion. I spoke to Athenagoras last night at a party about the latest 'message'; of course, it would be unfair to let him 'carry the can' alone. I would be glad to have your opinion.

David Kennedy's answer arrived on 10 March:

"Thank you for letting me see the evidence in the Nektarios business. As you say it is mostly the 'Matthew' evidence which presents solid material here.

Kephalas Nektarios—this indeed was his name and some of this information is available to anyone looking up the Penguin Dictionary of Saints. His feast day is indeed the 9th November. Kephalas Nektarios did indeed begin the building of a nunnery (not a monastery) in Aegina and I believe his tomb is in Aegina. He was also rector of the Rhizarion College. The above information is available to anyone using a library.

This information is therefore not to be discounted but held in the context of the other material, in the knowledge that it does not require a supernormal explanation to account for it.

Only Athenagoras can speak to the personal deatils of:

(1) Hieronymos.
(2) The displeasure from Chrysostomos and Athens.
(3) The 8,000 in Aegina.
(4) Zoë.
(5) Eusebius Matthopoulos and Makrakis.

Incidentally, regarding the message from Makrakis that the answer will be found in the Book of Revelation, may I suggest one interpretation of this cryptic message. Athenagoras is Archbishop of Thyateira and Thyateira is one of the seven churches to whom the risen Christ addresses Himself in the Book of Revelation. It is to Thyateira that the words are spoken "I know thy works—the last to be more than the first". Could this be a message for Athenagoras?

If the items which could not be available to Matthew in any form, turn out to be (1) True in fact. (2) True also to the situation of Athenagoras. (3) In keeping also with the character and wishes of Kephalas Nektarios as he is remembered—then we have something. Such evidence would be worth presenting to any student of parapsychology as highly persuasive evidence that Kephalas Nektarios is in fact trying to get through."

I subsequently spoke to Archbishop Athenagoras. His Eminence had requested to see the message which contained references to *Eusebius Matthopoulos* and *Makrakis*. There was no doubt that the particular message bothered the Archbishop. He admitted to having known Eusebius Matthopoulos and added that Matthopoulos and Makrakis had been friends of Nektarios. But what puzzled him most was the reference to Makrakis and the Book of Revelation. It appears that the Synod from which Athenagoras had returned had concerned itself to some degree with Makrakis and his interpretation of the Book of Revelation. The Archbishop could not reveal any more details, but he expressed his complete surprise at the latest message from Nektarios.

Since then there have been two further messages directly addressed to Archbishop Athenagoras. Both contain directives with regard to the monastery which Nektarios wants to see built in Britain.

Matthew describes Nektarios as a strong, and impatient comunicator. *The Psychic Researcher* will in due course arrange a meeting between Mrs. Katsikides and Matthew Manning in the presence of Archbishop Athenagoras, possibly at St. Nektarios' Church in Battersea. Whether or not such a meeting will yield unusual results remains to be seen.

The last two messages from Nektarios are obviously addressed to Matthew personally:

"Soon you will be with a spirit close to you who will produce for me a drawing which will be used in connection with my monastery. Keep it and when it is completed I shall my intentions reveal ot you. We here are all behind you and now I have chosen you to help raise funds.
Blessings

Kephalas Nektarios†"

After the picture had been "received", two days later, Nektarios gave long and detailed instructions about its use. It is to be published in "the book" and to be given to Athenagoras.

For the first time, a reference to Mrs. Katsikides appears:

"Mostly will Coula receive instructions from me . . ."

and the message to Matthew concludes:

"Although you may love no material object you will be rewarded by us. Quick now. Blessings Kephalas Nektarios†. Already you have had enough proof of my existence. Go to Athenagoras if you must see it. I am concerned only with my job now."

Apart from Matthew's involvement in this case, I have gathered evidence which has not been mentioned in this report. It is certainly remarkable that Kephalas Nektarios, who died in 1920 and was made a Saint in the Greek Orthodox Church in 1961, appears to have "communicated" through many different channels over the last few years. Matthew Manning, whose automatic writing is the prime concern of this report, is only one of several people who, quite independently from one another, seem to receive instructions from Nektarios.

On Sunday, 16 June 1974, His Eminence Archbishop Athenagoras Greek Orthodox Metropolitan of Great Britain discussed the implications of the evidence laid before him which indicated that the late Bishop Nektarios had on several occasions addressed himself to His Eminence.

This evidence was tentatively evaluated in context with other evidence purporting to originate from Nektarios and which had been received mainly through Mrs. Coula Katsikides of Battersea, London

In view of the overwhelming veneration the Greek Orthodox Saint has received in the past two years, His Eminence will consecrate the Church of St. Nektarios on 6 October 1974.

After elaborating on the events relating to Mrs. Katsikides, His Eminence dealt with the automatic writings received through Matthew Manning; several of his statements were in answer to questions.

Archbishop Athenagoras:

"The case of Matthew Manning is beyond any form of logical investigation. I can say positively that the young man has been in no position to know of certain things which were contained in those 'letters'. My own link to Saint Nektarios is through my teacher; he was ordained a deacon by Nektarios and was his pupil. Matthopoulo was, in fact a close friend of Nektarios, and the reference to Makrakis is absolutely amazing. This particular 'message' was received by Matthew when I was in Athens attending a most secret synod of Metropolitans. I cannot say more than that Makrakis was discussed at the synod and so was his book on the Book of Revelation. Having declared Makrakis an apostate because his views have always been rather against any reconciliation with the Roman Catholic Church on theological grounds, it is absolutely astonishing how Matthew could have known about this, because all these matters were discussed in camera, roughly at the time when Matthew received the message

"Aegina, its monastery and monastic order were the creation of Nektarios. The Saint has always been most ecumenically minded during his lifetime. Why he wants a monastery in England to twin the one in Aegina, I don't know, but it makes sense.

"Why should Nektarios send 'messages' to me through the hand of an 'outsider'? I don't know but I have always accepted that God has many ways in sending messages to His people—even to his bishops. And let us admit—even today we don't understand the meaning of many prophecies of old.

"I can only judge these messages on one ground: do they make sense?—

As I said, it makes sense to have a centre for ecumenical work; it makes sense to have a centre where we could train our young people for the new kind of work the Church has to face.

"However, I also must look at this from a different angle: for example, I cannot ask people for money to build such a monastery. I have recently launched an urgent appeal to buy four Churches in London. So the question of an appeal for money must be ruled out. All appeals for money contain an element of profitism—and even the suspicion of using this material for profit—however worthy—must be avoided.

"I also have to consider some other points: A monastery needs money but even more important, a monastery needs people. Who are the people who would join this monastery? Are they men or women? Again, one could suggest that people need a monastery . . . , however, these are thoughts which have to be considered.

"But I am sufficiently impressed with the evidence to say this: If there are people who want to help towards the realisation of the project Saint Nektarios wants, let those people write to me. I am willing to listen. I go further, I am prepared to support this project personally and I am willing to work with them on the establishment of the monastery. I would be prepared to appoint someone to investigate the possibility of finding a property.

"The appeal from Nektarios has come—to a large extent—from Matthew Manning who is not a Greek Orthodox Christian; it has come from outside, so to speak. Perhaps it is the intention of Saint Nektarios that outsiders should take a special interest in this project?

"I am fully in favour of taking into full consideration all that has been laid before me in evidence. Of course, this is a matter to be considered by those who are interested in Spiritual matters. This is not a matter to be put, say, before the Officials of the Church, as one would place the annual accounts before a committee of officials. Here we have something which concerns a service to and by the people of God; so let us leave the officials out of it for the time being. Here we deal with the development of Christian ecumenical activity.

"In principle, I will act whenever there is a sound source of information; I consider the evidence laid before me sound because it makes sense. Therefore I am prepared to investigate the claims. The soundness must be based on historical witness. We must co-ordinate all the information we have received and we must somehow be told clearly what the purpose is of this institution.

"I am therefore prepared to listen to all those who wish to express their opinion, offer help or advise. If I receive sufficient letters from readers,* for example, I shall, of course, appoint a committee to investigate what should be done. Personally, I am impressed by what I have seen—especially if I take into consideration the many miraculous happenings attributed to Saint Nektarios. Let the people judge on the strength of the evidence available. I am prepared to listen and give my support when it is needed."

* His Eminence Archbishop Athenagoras died on 9 September 1979.

APPENDIX II

DR. GEORGE OWEN

Report by Dr. A. R. G. Owen, Fellow of Trinity College, Cambridge.
Geneticist, Biologist and Mathematician.
Director "The New Horizons Research Foundation" Toronto.

LET ME SAY at the outset that I regard Matthew Manning as a most exciting person. This is an account of the extraordinary talents he is endowed with—talents, which for want of a better word, we call "psychic". They are so called because they seem to be related to the mind or soul of their possessor. Consequently we use the word "psychic" which derives from the Greek *psyche* meaning soul or mind and appears in *psychology, psychiatry,* etc. The terms *psychic* or *psychical* are however used in a more restricted way to embrace various mental phenomena such as telepathy or thought-transference. The word telepathy has passed into everyday life and hardly needs explanation, but there seem to be other strange phenomena which occur to many people, and are called clairvoyance and precognition. These too are embraced by the term *psychic*. The study of such events is spoken of as psychical research, a term first introduced in 1882 when the Society for Psychical Research was founded by three Fellows of Trinity College, Cambridge. Professor Henry Sidgwick, Frederick Myers, and Edmund Gurney. Historically Cambridge has had a long connection with psychical research. It was therefore not entirely accidental that I became acquainted with the Manning family.

As a result of contact with my senior colleague at Trinity, the eminent philosopher, Professor C. D. Broad, I in my turn had become interested in psychical research, parapsychology (as it is also called). One thing led to another and in 1967 when Derek Manning telephoned me at the college I had for several years devoted a large proportion of my spare time to psychical research. Especially I had interested myself in a particular kind of phenomenon known as poltergeist disturbances and had published a rather long book on the subject (*Can We Explain the Poltergeist?*, Taplinger Publishing Co., New York), in which I examined this phenomenon from every angle. Usually a poltergeist disturbance is of limited duration. The phenomena disappear after an interval of days or weeks. More rarely they may last for some months, but this is unusual. Once they subside they usually never recur, which was the basis of the firm declaration which I made to this effect in 1967.

During the last two centuries or more, hundreds of poltergeist cases have been written up, often by very good witnesses independent of the family most immediately concerned. As a result there is no doubt whatever that most of them are completely genuine. By this I mean to say that the events which are said to occur actually do occur and are not the result of hallucination or mass hypnotism. If strange noises occur they can be recorded on a tape-recorder. If a vase appears to be smashed then it really is smashed; one has merely to pick up the pieces. It is true also in a vast majority of cases that the phenomena are not due to anyone playing tricks. However, to know this one has to have spent a great deal of time studying these phenomena. The subject is getting better known of late as a result of my own efforts and those of distinguished investigators such as Professor Hans Bender, Dr. Gaither Pratt, and Mr. William Roll. But the public at large are as yet not fully informed and any person experiencing a poltergeist outbreak is naturally chary of telling outsider about it.

One of the most common types of happening in poltergeist cases is the occurrences of unusual and inexplicable noises. Of course every house, whether new or old, is likely to be rich in natural sounds due to such causes as expansion or shrinking of timbers, water in the pipes, or underground. However in a large proportion of poltergeist cases the sounds are quite unmistakable for anything else. They can be scratching or sawing noises or loud insistent raps coming out of the woodwork of furniture, or out of the walls, or even sometimes appearing to originate in thin air! It is because of these noises that the name "poltergeist" became attached to these disturbances. Poltergeist is an old German folklore word made up of *polter* (noise) and *geist* (spirit), so that it means "noise-sprite" and was used in the Middle Ages to refer to hypothetical nature spirits (the German equivalent of our own elves, goblins, brownies etc.) who were supposed to be mischievous without meaning real harm—like Shakespeare's Puck. However it is not clear at all that poltergeist happenings are due to a spirit and so as not to beg the question it is best not to refer to poltergeists in this connection but instead to speak only of "poltergeist disturbances", or, as I do, of "poltergeistery".

In some instances of poltergeistery the only phenomena are sounds. Occasionally the sounds occur very frequently many times in a day. In other cases they happen very intermittently. Sometimes several days pass between phenomena. Some poltergeist outbreaks have no noises at all but only movement of objects. A poltergeist case at Swansea in Wales which occurred a year or so before I met Matthew opened with a medicine bottle rising off a shelf and floating towards the lady of the house. She retreated in alarm, shutting the door in the face of the advancing bottle, which hit it with an audible crash. In a case at Sauchie, Alloa, Scotland, in 1960, two doctors and a minister testified that on more than one occasion they had seen a heavy linen chest rise an inch or two off the floor and then float along in the air for a distance of some feet. The Sauchie case, besides having frequent movements of objects also had a rich profusion of loud raps and other noises (which were tape-recorded). The doctors said these often seemed to come from points in mid-air. However, in the Swansea outbreak as in many others, there were no "paranormal" sounds; objects moved silently until they struck on other objects in which case, of course, there was the noise of impact. But these collision noises were, of course, normal sounds—the only abnormal feature was the motion of the objects which we have described as "paranormal". This is a convenient word to apply to happenings which we cannot explain in terms of known natural forces. It is a better word to use than "supernatural" because we cannot be certain that phenomena of this type do not result from the operation of forces that are completely natural and in the future may be understood even if we do not understand them at the present time.

The Swansea case (see Andrew Mackenzie's book: *The Unexplained*, Arthur Barker Ltd., London, 1966) was interesting as it showed how powerful the poltergeist force can be. On one occasion a double bed was lifted up by the force, turned upside down and deposited on top of a baby's cot. Shortly before or after this occurred a heavy wardrobe in the same room was moved so as to obstruct the only door leading in or out of the bedroom. The police had to be fetched to the scene to effect an entrance into the room which was on the first floor facing the street. While these events were going on the lady of the house and her mother were standing on the pavement below the window. It was therefore clear that no housebreaker or hooligan had caused the upheaval in the bedroom because he could not have escaped unobserved. The Swansea disturbance also illustrates a feature found in many poltergeist cases; objects will be moved inside closed rooms when no one is there, and the fact is only discovered afterwards. This "slyness" as it were, has been so often reported that I regard it as a quite typical feature of poltergeist disturbances.

The immediate cause of any individual happening in a poltergeist outbreak is, of course, the exertion of a physical force of unknown nature. If a bed weighing 200 pounds is lifted into the air then a force of at least 200 pounds weight is being exerted. If a rapping noise is coming out of the woodwork of a table, then we know that the molecules of the wood at the place of origin of the sound are being set into vibration and this too implies the operation of a force. What is the cause of this force? Some people approach the problem in much the same way as did the Germans in the Middle Ages, and ascribe all poltergeist and like phenomena to the direct action of spirits, either the spirits of the dead, or to imps and demons. On this theory it is a discarnate being (of one species or the other) that is exerting the physical force on objects.

In trying to decide whether or not this could be the true explanation, the investigator of an outbreak of poltergeistery will first try to establish whether or not the happenings are always confined to a single building. If so, the situation might be that of the so-called "haunted house". Haunted house situations are usually very complex and difficult to analyse (see my book *Science and the Spook*, Dobson, London). Contrary to popular belief visible "ghosts" or apparitions are not the essential and invariable feature of haunted house situations, a surprisingly large proportion of which involve physical phenomena of poltergeist type.

Often it is found that poltergeistery is not attached to a particular building but instead occurs only when one particular member of the family is nearby. The Sauchie case, already mentioned, was a perfect example of this. Events happened in the home of an eleven-year-old girl, Virginia. She was sent to stay with her aunt in another town, but things were as bad as ever; so she came home and went to school. In the class-room desks rose into the air and a heavy table was pushed across the floor to the surprise of the school-teacher. Every paranormal physical event that happened took place within a few feet from Virginia. For this reason the simplest explanation is to suppose that the force which moved the furniture and which made the raps was in some way operated by Virginia herself. A great many other recorded poltergeist cases have fallen into exactly this pattern; the phenomena are attached to a person and not to a place. It is convenient to describe this type of case as being one of "classic" or "pure" type, to distinguish it from the haunted house situation.

Of course, the fact that in a case of pure or classic type, the phenomena are attached to a single person does not, in itself, prove absolutely that a discarnate spirit is not also involved as well as the poltergeist person (i.e. Virginia in the Sauchie outbreak). One theory is that there is, in fact, a discarnate spirit but that he, she, or it cannot produce the phenomena by themselves. On this theory the poltergeist person is someone who is endowed with a special "psychic" talent which enables them to be used by a disembodied spirit as a

164

kind of intermediary or link, facilitating the manifestation of actions of the spirit. Proponents of this theory speak of the poltergeist person as a "medium" meaning an intermediary between the physical world and the spirits. The word *medium* in this sense was in use certainly as early as 1852, during the first years of the spread of the spiritualist movement. As a matter of interest it is worth remarking that modern Spiritualism was stimulated into being by an outburst of polter-geistery involving rapping noises which occurred in the presence of two teenage girls, the Fox sisters of Hydesville, in New York State, U.S.A.

I will defer until later any discussion of the concept of mediumship in its many forms. For the present it is sufficient to say that in a large proportion of classic poltergeist cases there is no real evidence that the central person is functioning as a medium for spirit communica-tion. Firstly we note that in "pure" poltergeist cases it is rare for apparitions of the dead to be seen by the poltergeist person himself or by the bystanders. Similarly none of the persons concerned seem to receive by way of mental impressions any purported messages from the deceased or from any other beings. Nor do they go into "mediumistic trances", or seem, while the phenomena are happen-ing, to be in a state of consciousness other than their normal one. Similarly many of the conditions traditionally supposed necessary in spiritualist seances for physical phenomena to happen, e.g. darkness and the presence of a circle of sympathetic people just do not apply in poltergeist cases. Phenomena occur in full light and are apt to disconcert even the most hostile and sceptical observers. Also, for what it is worth, we may note that "ectoplasm"—a subtle form of matter, supposed to exude from the medium's body, has never been seen in any poltergeist case of classic type. Finally we may note that in such outbreaks it is usually difficult or impossible to recognise any attempt at communication.

Because of the reasons I have mentioned and also the difference between the classic poltergeist case and the haunted house situation, many serious students of the subject (and this includes people who also accept that in other contexts spirit communication does take place) believe that the typical poltergeist outbreak results from the involuntary deployment by the poltergeist person of a special form of psychic ability with which he is endowed. This is the capacity for psycho-kinesis or P.K. as it is called for short. In poltergeist cases it seems to be quite outside of the conscious control of the poltergeist person. He or she is usually quite as puzzled and disconcerted by the happenings as everyone else, and genuinely surprised when at last it appears from observation that their presence has something to do with the occurrence of the phenomena.

Is there any other evidence that a P.K. force exists? It seems that many ordinary people can exert this power voluntarily but only in a very minute degree. The evidence for this is the large number of experiments on influencing the fall of dice, a research instituted by Professor Joseph B. Rhine at Duke University, North Carolina, U.S.A. It has been found that when dice are thrown randomly by a mechanical method, persons who consciously will that they fall with a chosen side uppermost, e.g. a "three", can produce a slight tendency for the dice to fall as required. This only shows up statistically; thus, the degree of voluntary control is somewhat limited. A few gifted individuals can produce somewhat bigger effects. Thus my friend Jan Merta in Canada can regulate the movement of a mobile hung inside an air-proof jar. Mme. Mikhailova, a Russian lady, can move small objects such as cigarette lighters, matchboxes and matches for short distances over the surface of a table. Mr. Merta and Mme. Mikhailova of course, have the psycho-kinetic power to a much greater degree than most people do. At the same time one has to say that their effects are much weaker than those encountered in many poltergeist cases. However it is an important fact that a few people, like Jan Merta, and Mme. Mikhailova, do exhibit the P.K. ability. It is logical therefore to suppose that it is this same power that is manifested temporarily by poltergeist persons.

When I first met Matthew and his family in 1966 I was quite familiar with the kind of phenomena to be expected in a typical poltergeist case. Also I was quite experienced in assessing the truthfulness of witnesses to poltergeist events. I soon formed the opinion that, in virtue of his profession, background, and manifest qualities, Mr. Manning was a highly factual and reliable witness. I therefore accepted that the phenomena which were said to happen in the mornings in the living room did in fact take place just as described with the whole family having tea upstairs under the eye of Mr Manning. Also the movement of the objects in the living room seemed to me to be quite in character with what has been reported in numerous poltergeist cases. The articles, some of them of great artistic merit, were always uninjured. This squares with what is found in the vast run of poltergeist outbreaks; treasured articles are not ruined; no person is seriously injured; it is as if the phenomena are designed to intrigue and to annoy rather than to injure people either bodily or in their feelings. The stealthiness of the phenomena was another feature which has frequently been noted. Consequently

166

I was disappointed but not surprised that nothing happened in the room during my vigils gazing into it from the garden.

The house was only a few years old and it seemed unlikely that it was haunted. Matthew has described how the three children were for a week dispersed to separate homes. If there had been phenomena at any of these residences it would have been helpful, as it would have afforded some clue as to which member or members of the family were psycho-kinetic persons. I felt certain that at least one person was manifesting P.K. powers. The probabilities were that the ability was restricted to only one of them. Also, on the basis of statistics got from the study of very many poltergeist cases, the most likely candidate for this distinction was Matthew. It has been found that poltergeist persons tend to be between 10 and 20 years old. Matthew was the most likely on grounds of age. Also some degree of tension or anxiety seems to be contributory to poltergeist activity. As he himself has mentioned, he was in the last lap of preparing for an important examination. However these were all mere probabilities and not certainties. Poltergeist phenomena do sometimes centre on younger children or on adults. To this day I am not sure why Mr. and Mrs. Manning noticed noises in the house during the absence of the children. As the family eventually moved to another town this will doubtless remain unsolved. Possibly the house always had a tendency to structural noises which obtruded themselves on the family's attention only after the poltergeist happenings had alerted them to the possibility of paranormal happenings and so induced a state of heightened auditory awareness. In any case I felt sufficiently confident that this was a classic poltergeist case and not a haunted house situation, as to assert that the house was not haunted. I explained also that with high probability the phenomena resulted from the involuntary functioning of P.K. ability by some member of the family. Finally I declared that the phenomena would fade out after some weeks, as in fact they did, though not before some variations of the phenomena had occurred, and which Matthew has mentioned. The "pinging" sound as of the impact of a small bead on a solid surface has been described in many poltergeist cases. The feeling of pressure, as if a small animal was walking over the bedcovers, which Mr. Manning experienced also has its counterpart in former cases. I do not doubt the reality of either of these types of occurrence.

In the great majority of poltergeist cases there is a single outbreak which eventually subsides after a few days or weeks. Only rarely does the person concerned later manifest any psychic abilities of either the mental or psychokinetic type. Consequently the likelihood is that a poltergeist disturbance will never be repeated in the same family. However there have been a few exceptions to this rule. For instance, Mme. Mikhailova, whom I have mentioned, was as a young woman the centre of strong poltergeistery, domestic utensils leaping from the shelves of her kitchen. She came to the attention of Professor Vasiliev an eminent Soviet physiologist, who suggested that she seek to train herself so as to be able to operate consciously her P.K. power. In this she was moderately successful and by mental concentration she can move small selected objects. It would seem therefore that a small proportion of poltergeist people are more permanently endowed with the potentiality for psychokinetic power. Consequently they are more likely than the rest to have a recurrence, especially in times of stress which, we have noted, are for some mysterious reason conducive to manifestation of the P.K. ability. Though, like most poltergeist persons, they are in other respects normal (indeed, it would seem, a a group somewhat above the normal, being of more than average intelligence and in their behaviour rather well-behaved), this continuing latent ability makes them very interesting people, because the psychokinetic ability is indeed a very amazing one.

When therefore in the Spring of 1971 Mr. Manning wrote to tell me that Matthew was the centre of new and much more varied and powerful poltergeistery, I was not totally astonished, but I was surprised and also intrigued by the probability that in Matthew we had a person of outstanding psychic ability. However there was still the question of his career at school and after, and I was mainly concerned with exerting such little influence as I could exert from Canada to minimise any ill consequences these events would have in respect of Matthew's career. I therefore wrote to the Headmaster in as authoritative and persuasive a style as I was capable of, to underline the fact that Matthew was not an irresponsible mischief maker, but as much a victim of an uninvited situation as the school staff and boys were. I hope that I did some good; as the reader is aware, it was a near thing! However the Headmaster acted with discretion and humanity just as did the Headmaster of Sauchie School when presented with Virginia's phenomena. I might say, in parenthesis, that though these cases are uncommon, they are not exceptionally rare; every person in charge of children or juveniles ought to receive as part of his professional training some instruction in the recognition and management of poltergeist outbreaks. I think with more prior knowledge the staff of Matthew's school could have regulated the whole affair so that it would have been much less upsetting to all concerned. However all's well that ends well! Tragedy averted has a habit, at least in retrospect, of turning into comedy and readers must have appreciated the humorous aspects of Matthew's excellently written account of the happenings at school. I can testify that this account differs in no particular from what Matthew and his father reported to us at the time. It is an unembellished narrative in no way heightened or exaggerated in the recollection.

I believe Matthew's narrative is a true account. I say this despite the remarkable nature of some of the phenomena. Most of the happenings are paralleled in other poltergeist cases where they have been described by unchallengeable witnesses, and so, though strange, they are perfectly possible. Also the witnesses, some of them reluctant and hostile but all independent of the Manning family, were too numerous for there to be any doubt on the matter. As Matthew has said, his second run of poltergeistery opened in July 1970. Occurrences like those of the flying boot and self-opening wardrobe and the scratching noises are the small change of poltergeistery and in that context hardly remarkable, but they serve to date the re-emergence from latency of Matthew's psycho-kinetic powers. During the rest of the winter they were comparatively muted. The episode of the pen, which repeatdly disappeared from the desk in his study to be found elsewhere, at first sight appears to be merely the phenomenon of sly movement of small objects. However it may actually have entailed a more awesome phenomenon, the moving of objects out of closed rooms or into closed rooms. This is known as teleportation. The episode of the torch, which during the Easter vacation, was found inexplicably inside the (presumably closed) pantry also hints at this strange phenomenon which I discuss later.

Easter Sunday 1971 initiated a faster tempo of events in which the contents of rooms at the Manning home were disarranged on a large scale, reminding us of the Swansea case. A truly notable aspect of these upheavals is that they took place at high speed, rooms being put into disarray in a matter of minutes, but the agency at work exhibited a remarkable delicacy. Though physical forces of the order of thirty or so pounds weight were applied in lifting pieces of furniture, these objects were deposited so lightly as to do no damage. This may seem almost incredible but is paralleled in numerous cases and clearly indicates a certain considerateness or inhibition which acts to minimize real injury. The delicate balancing feats which Matthew describes are also paralleled elsewhere and illustrate the same marvellous precision of which the psychokinetic force is capable. At his stage the Manning family experienced another interesting feature I have noticed in poltergeistery: the way in which the phenomena can be modified by suggestion. Apparently the family temporarily shunted the phenomena into specializing in electrical appliances and later taps. The latter suggestion was, perhaps, not entirely a happy one as it preceded, and possibly induced, a series of phenomena relating to transport of fluids—acid, ink, paint stripper and caustic soda. As I cannot imagine that in the Manning household these liquids were not kept in closed bottles, this would seem to indicate a further occurrence of the mysterious phenomena of teleportation. In some respects these episodes resembled the outbreak at another place in East Anglia, namely the Rectory at Swanton Novers, Suffolk. This was in 1919 and liquids such as oil or water ran out of the walls and ceilings. This strange occurrence was testified to by numerous press reporters as well as an architect, a geologist, a chemist and a couple of oil engineers, as well as by John Maskelyne, the famous illusionist.

Though some readers may find it mind-boggling, I accept as totally possible Matthew's statement that Rosalind's table vanished from her room and (either simultaneously or later) was deposited in the cellar. My reason for believing that teleportation is possible is as follows. When in 1962 I made my survey of poltergeist reports I found that in at least fifty cases, poltergeist phenomena of the more "ordinary" kind (e.g. flights of objects, etc.) were accompanied by instances of articles disappearing from closed rooms or locked containers. Sometimes these items would reappear elsewhere. Often they were seen in the act of reappearing. Very commonly, small articles such as coins or pebbles were said to appear suddenly in mid-air. The same was often said of objects which had never been in the house in question and which seemingly had originated elsewhere. In many of the 50 cases these phenomena of teleportation or apportation were testified to by very respectable witnesses. When I wrote *Can We Explain the Poltergeist?* I said, therefore, that, difficult as it was to credit the phenomenon, the evidence for it was too persuasive for it to be rejected out of hand and the problem ought therefore to "lie on the table". Since 1962 many other instances have been described. Unfortunately no parapsychologist has so far observed the phenomenon in poltergeist cases under conditions sufficiently rigorous as to leave absolutely no doubt of its occurrence, but I am inclined to think that it is only a matter of time before a definitive observation eventuates. In recent months teleportation has frequently been reported as occurring sporadically among Mr. Uri Geller's phenomena. I understand that some scientific experiments have actually been done in which objects have vanished from sealed boxes, but official scientific reports have not yet been published. It would be fair to say that while teleportation and apportation are not yet fully established as scientific facts, none-the-less there exists a strong presumption that sometimes they do occur. Consequently we can give credence to Matthew's description of the appearance of small objects in the School Matron's Office as if coming from nowhere. Similarly, the articles thrown in the dormitory may well have originated outside the room.

Thus, with one exception, the types of phenomena at Matthew's school, though unusual in frequency, power and variety, did not transgress the bounds of what has been reported in other poltergeist cases. However the appearances of the rings or discs of light on the walls are, as far as I know, unparalleled in poltergeistery. The only point of similarity to other cases is the fact that the luminous patches seemed to be heated. Now local heating of walls, wallpaper, bed-covers, and curtains has been noted in about a score of cases, often this has led to smouldering and even the heated material actually burning. This has been regarded as paranormal because it is not at all easy to ignite wallpaper by ordinary means. But the luminosity at the school seems to be a different phenomenon. It is interesting that Matthew felt it to be different. From his account it is clear that he worked out for himself that though his participation in all the preceding happenings had been unintended, involuntary, and out-side his conscious control, he was in some way the cause of them; they were an expression by unconscious means of an internal stress and tension. But he felt that the luminous circles were generated by a force outside himself which he described as spirit intervention. Interestingly enough, Matthew does not seem to feel that the scribbling on the walls at home and the writing of *Matthew Beware* indicated spirit communication. I imagine that in coming to this conclusion his reasoning resembled that which I would be inclined to apply to it; the childishly drawn loops and circles are inconsistent with the ability to spell out even so short a message as *Matthew Beware*. Also, this putative message seemed to be without actual reference as, in the event, nothing awful took place. This inconsis-tency and irrelevance are also typical of the writing on walls, or on paper, which has been reported in other poltergeist cases. Similarly when "messages" are received by other means in the course of polter-geist outbreaks, e.g. by coded rappings or even the "direct voice", the supposed "communicator" cannot be identified as a real person-lity. Often its communications and descriptions of itself are quite incoherent; "it" will give inconsistent and indeed contradictory accounts of who "it" is, or was. To my mind, this reinforces the view mentioned earlier that in classic or pure poltergeistery there is no real evidence of the intervention of spirits whether deceased human beings or any other kind of entity.

As I have said, the fact that Matthew after a lapse of years was the centre of continuing poltergeist activity on a grander scale is extremely interesting because it suggests that unlike the usual poltergeist person he is a highly endowed "psychic", as someone with continuing psychic abilities is often called. Mme. Mikhailova is an example of a psychic who permanently retained her P.K. talent but, so far as I am aware, does not exhibit mental abilities, i.e. telepathy, clairvoyance, or precognition. However I know of one or two psychic "sensitives" who are highly endowed with extrasensory perception; these are not P.K. persons but in their early years experienced a few psychokinetic events. One interesting case is described in the book *Beyond Belief.*

A completely normal young man, aged about thirty, was the centre of poltergeist activity when at work in his photography studio. This was followed by a phase in which he developed something akin to trance mediumship. After the sittings devoted to this were discontinued, he found that he was developing psychic abilities of the mental kind, particularly precognition—the prediction of events which could easily be foreseen. Thus I came to wonder if in certain cases poltergeistery is the first stage in the natural evolution of a powerful psychic. If this is so then Matthew would seem to exemplify a rare but important pattern of development. The experience of seeing the human aura which he reports is also one shared by many psychic sensitives though one which it is extremely difficult to interpret.

If the replacement of physical phenomena by mental psychic phenomena is a regular feature of a certain mode of psychic development, it is a most intriguing fact. In so far as the psychic person is unconsciously motivated it could be regarded as a substitution of a socially harmless activity in the place of a socially disruptive one—the irritating poltergeistery. It is most interesting that consciously Matthew strove to effect this substitution—guided by intellectual curiosity on the one hand and on the other by what may be described as enlightened self-interest, i.e. to make the phenomena socially innocuous, to minimize distress to his family and friends. Here the operative word is "enlightened"; as far as self-interest is concerned the world could do with an unlimited amount of the enlightened variety. I think myself it is a great credit to Matthew's intelligence and insight that he sought consciously to substitute activities in the sphere of mental sensitivity for the chaotic poltergeistery. If, as is possible, it shows that inchoate P.K. events can be replaced by mental abilities of the extrasensory kind, it is a very important finding— both practically and theoretically.

In passing it is worth commenting on the "ritual" of abolishing the poltergeistery recommended by the gentleman at the mental hospital. This ritual seems to be an item from the vast repertoire of occultist studies centred on the age-old practice of magic. For clarity, I had best say straightaway that I do not fear magic or witchcraft because I believe them to be nonsense cut out of the broadcloth of superstition and erroneous tradition. However, like Matthew, I have no appetite for them as I regard them as foolish and misleading, also via the great power of suggestion they can precipitate phobias, anxiety and neuroses among those credulous people who are intellectually incapable of rejecting the empty mumbo-jumbo in which these traditions abound. I should emphasise that these ill effects result entirely from natural psychological causes and not from supernatural efficacy of the rituals or doctrines. As we see from Matthew's account the ritual worked on the first occasion it was used but failed thereafter. This is just what we would expect from any procedure used to allay poltergeistery. At the first application it may (possibly, but not certainly), have effect, but often after a decent interval the phenomena recur. This is in accordance with psychology; psychological factors may produce the desired subsidence of events for a time. But every instrument becomes blunted with use. There is a close parallel with exorcism or services of prayer or intervention. The effects tend to be temporary only. This is also true of many instances of the particular kind of "faith healing" which depends on psychological factors only.

Much more significant is the success of Matthew's own efforts to channel or canalise his powers into purely mental phenomena (for automatic writing and drawing fall into this category). It seems too early to assess whether in all cases of automatic writing by Matthew the information was paranormally acquired. This would need a great deal of historical research. Matthew himself expresses a fairly conservative view when he alludes to the possibility of a contribution from his own unconscious (e.g. either subconscious phantasy or his memory bank). However I think it unlikely that Matthew (book-lover as he is) would write South Arabian Arabic. I am no cook, and can give no opinion as to the type of culinary advice that would be appropriate to Mrs. Beeton, but I was intrigued by the material relating to Sir Stafford Cripps, who was my own M.P. at Bristol. I followed his career with interest but knew nothing of Sapperton or Frith Hill. Without committing myself on the question, which deserves exhaustive and complete study, I am inclined to say there is quite a case for supposing that Matthew receives information by paranormal means. Whether this is actually from the spirits of the dead I cannot say. Evidence for human survival of death from automatic writing or by other means of communication has been discussed extensively during the last half-century. It is a field in which I am myself not competent to give a worth-while opinion. I respect those who have examined the whole body of evidence for human survival of death and have felt able to come up with an affirmative conclusion. But I also respect those students who argue that the power of extrasensory perception is almost unlimited. This latter school of thought suggests that a powerful psychic can acquire a remarkable amount of accurate knowledge by extrasensory perception, perhaps by telepathy from the living or by the faculty which, for want of a better word, is called clairvoyance. Whichever interpretation one chooses to adopt there remain many mysteries and loose ends.

I am especially intrigued by the recent indication that Matthew is to some degree capable of developing new physical phenomena. Lately, in regard to other psychics I have tended to suspect that their talents are potentially psychologically malleable. In a recent interview Mr. Uri Geller said that he tended to restrict himself to seeking to produce only certain types of phenomena such as his effects on watches and the bending and division of metal. He thought that possibly this was because these were the phenomena that he first had in his youth. He therefore had faith that they would work and so these were the ones he sought to produce. It is fascinating therefore that Matthew has been able, when fired by Uri's example, to produce his own metal phenomena. I should say, in passing, that very recently my wife received what, for us, was absolute proof of the validity of Uri's metal phenomena. A key in my wife's purse which Uri had never handled or even seen, and which was examined by a committee of witnesses before being put into the purse, was bent through 30 degrees while still in the purse with Uri at least 25 feet away. I started this commentary by saying that Matthew is an exciting person. This is so not only because of his remarkable abilities but on account of his reflective and detached attitude to them. Many psychic persons content themselves with mere repetition of their paranormal effects and this perhaps is one of the reasons why parapsychology advances only slowly. But if Matthew can continue to combine the exercise of his powers with the same spirit of enquiry that he has already shown, it is likely that his work may lead to a new and profound scientific insight into these matters.

INDEX

Page numbers in italics indicate illustrations

INDEX

Page numbers in italics indicate illustrations